26 LETTERS BUT STUCK ON Y

WHY ME?
WHY THIS?
WHY NOW?
A WAY FORWARD AMIDST THE STRUGGLE

TYLER WHITCOMB

WESTBOW
P R E S S®
A DIVISION OF THOMAS NELSON
& ZONDERVAN

WestBow Press books may be ordered through booksellers or by contacting:

WestBow Press
A Division of Thomas Nelson & Zondervan
1663 Liberty Drive
Bloomington, IN 47403
www.westbowpress.com
844-714-3454

Scripture taken from the Holy Bible, NEW INTERNATIONAL
VERSION®, NIV® Copyright © 1973, 1978, 1984, 2011 by Biblica,
Inc.® Used by permission. All rights reserved worldwide.

ISBN: 978-1-6642-9984-9 (sc)
ISBN: 978-1-6642-9983-2 (e)

Library of Congress Control Number: 2023908890

Print information available on the last page.

WestBow Press rev. date: 08/25/2023

Dedicated to my wife, Karen for believing in the goodness of God even when life is hard.

ENDORSEMENTS

I love when people who love Jesus love people!

Tyler is one of those people. As you read this book, you will feel seen and cared for, by God and by Tyler. I did ! Tyler tackles some of the hardest questions that we all carry around like barbells stuffed into our backpacks, and he addresses them with deep thoughts, and fresh views from the Bible, and from personal experiences that are not unlike yours. I appreciate that Tyler doesn't separate himself from us, he's a fellow strugglers in this journey and he's thought a great deal about what it all means. This book reminded me how humanity is still struggling with the same pains, and searching to make sense of our circumstances and confusion. These uncertainties are not going away, but neither is the God who made you and loves you and feels your pain and your wonder!

Thank you, Tyler, for this gift to me and to all who will be touched and encouraged. I envision all who will pick this book up, or pull it up on their digital device. Whoever and wherever you are, you will feel hope and optimism that God loves you and your life has greater meaning than you have imagined.

– Steve Andrews
Founding Pastor of Kensington Church

Tyler addresses a hard subject of pain and its cause(s), but he does so out of his own time of suffering physical and emotional set backs. Tyler's presentation style is a folksy and down to earth modern day language easy to understand. This book does not sugar coat the problems of suffering and pain with Christian-eze. I love the phrase, "Right theology does not diminish the pain of loss, right theology just does not allow you to be crushed by pain." I love his insights when he says, "We feel the way we do during suffering because we are human. And the world is a broken place, and it is not wrong to feel the emotions that we do. But when these feelings rise to the place of doubting God, we have to submit our feelings and inform our feelings of truth."

Tyler's hope for you as you read this book is that it "helps to deepen your understanding of God in the midst of suffering." My prayer is that his presentation of Scripture will help you do so.

– Dr. Bill Hossler
Pastor and former Missionary Church Denominational President

INTRODUCTION

I would imagine that a book like the one you are presently reading is one that would intrigue and speak to individuals who have experienced some form of the devastating pain that living in our world makes us accustomed to. Conversely, perhaps you are a skeptic, one who ponders the deep matters of the cosmos and yet attempts to shield yourself from all the pain and suffering in our world. Maybe you do not bother worrying about the root of the ups and downs of life and make attempts of denying the reality of God. If you fall into the first group, I'm sure there have been many sleepless nights, tossing and turning and truly questioning, "Why?" Why me? Why this? Why now?

For me, the desire to write on this topic of "why" was birthed out of my own story, my own hurt, and my own confusion. Because of my story, I had determined to go on a quest to truly begin asking questions about God, about suffering, about how to reconcile those things. I began devouring books, and I watched sermons and dove into scripture because certainly there must be answers to all of these questions. Some of the books that have influenced me are: The Problem of Pain by C.S. Lewis, Trusting God: Even When Life Hurts by Jerry Bridges. I do not pretend to be the greatest of sufferers, nor do I pretend to have the hardest of stories. In all honesty, I have had a good life, free of pain and suffering for much of it but certainly not all of it. Much of my story around suffering was birthed out of a diagnosis (Crohn's Disease) at the age of sixteen years old and a surgery at the age of nineteen related to that diagnosis which resulted in two months of hospital stay.

There are a few things I have learned in my lifetime that are certain:

- God is real (we'll get more into this later)
- Michigan is pure (thanks, Tim Allen)
- The Detroit Lions football team will never be Superbowl champs (do I sound like a jaded fan?)
- If you live long enough, you will experience pain (Ecclesiastes 12:1 NIV)

As you read that last line, let that set in. That is what Solomon says:

> Remember your Creator in the days of your youth,
> before the days of trouble come and the years approach
> when you will say,
> "I find no pleasure in them"— (Ecclesiastes 12:1 NIV)

That is a sobering reality, is it not? That the scriptures would say that there are days coming, and not even just days but years are coming, that we would have never wished for. Have you been there? Have those days and years already arrived for you?

Maybe for you, you are longing for a spouse, and after years of prayer, there seem to be no prospects coming your way. Perhaps your situation is that you and your spouse are longing for a child, and in every direction you look, there is no answer. Or maybe you have experienced the heartache of loss; loss of a relationship, loss of a loved one, loss of a job or finances. It could be that you have experienced suffering from a disease, emotionally, mentally, or physically. These examples are all too real within the Church that I pastor. Every example I just listed were meetings I had in my office within the last month.

Pain is not foreign to the human experience, but it is abnormal. Let me explain what I mean—pain not being foreign is pretty self-explanatory. I feel like I could just write down "2020, Covid, Presidential Election, Riots" and move on. We see and experience pain all around us, and up until this point in my life, I have not yet met a person who would say that their life story was one where pain did not exist. And while pain and suffering are real and seemingly unavoidable (because I don't know who is looking for pain), it is abnormal in the sense that it wasn't supposed to be this way.

If we look at the Genesis account, this is what we see:

> *In the beginning God created the heavens and the earth. (Genesis 1:1 NIV)*

The Creator God, the one who transcends the heavens and the earth, created from nothing everything that is.

Over and over, God is creating in the Genesis account. All throughout chapter one, you'll see words like "And God said," "God created," "He also made," ...and accompanying each of the statements has an ending, "and it was good" or "it was so."

We see a Eutopia where pain, hardships, and suffering are not a part of the design. Perfection was the norm in Eden. A perfect God was governing a perfect creation. But clearly, something changed because what was once normal (perfection) is now no longer and what was absent (suffering) is now present.

We know what happened according to God's Word. It is not some mystery that we are guessing at. Genesis 3 tells us that Adam and Eve took from the tree that had been prohibited (3:6). The "good" creation rebels against a perfect and holy God, and now we see sin introduced to the narrative, and with sin, there are consequences—this is evidenced by a pronouncement made by God:

> *To the woman he said,*
>
> *"I will make your pains in childbearing very severe; with painful labor you will give birth to children.*

Your desire will be for your husband, and he will rule over you."

To Adam he said, "Because you listened to your wife and ate fruit from the tree about which I commanded you, 'You must not eat from it,'

"Cursed is the ground because of you; through painful toil you will eat food from it all the days of your life. It will produce thorns and thistles for you, and you will eat the plants of the field. By the sweat of your brow you will eat your food until you return to the ground, since from it you were taken; for dust you are and to dust you will return." Genesis 3:16-19 NIV

And that passage of scripture is why I said though pain is not foreign to the human experience, it is abnormal. Because of sin, everything has been fractured. Things are not as they should be. The design has been tampered with.

The apostle Paul would write this in Romans:

For the creation waits in eager expectation for the children of God to be revealed. For the creation was subjected to frustration, not by its own choice, but by the will of the one who subjected it, IN HOPE that the creation itself will be liberated from its bondage to decay and brought into the freedom and glory of the children of God. Romans 8:19-21 NIV

All of creation is not as it was intended. You can look out at a beautiful sunset or mountain foothills, gaze across the ocean, look up at the Milky Way, and as beautiful as all those things are, that sunset, or mountain range are both "eagerly waiting" to be restored, to be made more beautiful.

I'm sure that you have experienced the abnormal at this point in your life. It's important to understand that the abnormal is correlated to sin, but maybe not in the way you are thinking about that statement. Believe me. I do not prescribe to the idea that if you lie to someone, God's going to give you cancer. But I am saying that sickness, disease, and death only happen because we now live in a fallen, broken world, and sin has entered the cosmos.

And so, this is an interesting concept for us to grasp: because we live in a fallen, broken world, things that are the norm are still abnormal. It's important that we look through the proper lens to truly see and understand our world. Because things like sickness, pain and hardships fog the lenses through which we see and understand God's goodness and love, if we never get to the root problem, our lenses will remain foggy. We will continually ask "why" because it will be impossible for us to see clearly.

I am going to invite you on a little mini journey with me, where we will look to God's word for insight and clarity. Along the way, I'll share stories about how God's grace and plan were made visible to me. I pray no matter where you are in your faith journey, this will build your confidence in God's good plan.

CHAPTER 1

CAN GOD STAND TRIAL?

"God is too good to be unkind, too wise to be mistaken; and when you cannot trace His hand, you can trust His heart." Charles Spurgeon

Growing up, one of my favorite movies was Tommy Boy with Chris Farley, and within the movie—Chris Farley plays a character named Tommy Callahan Jr., and here is the premise of the movie-- Tommy must replace his deceased father within the family company Callahan Auto. So he goes on a sales trip to attempt to sell half of a million brake pads to save the company from folding. Tommy had, throughout the entirety of the movie, kept butchering a line that his father used within his own sales pitches, but at the end of the movie (not a spoiler, you have had decades now to see it), he finally gets the line right and makes the big sale, and the line is "you can get a good look at a T-bone by sticking your head up a bulls *rear end* but wouldn't you rather take the butchers word for it." Now ultimately, that line is silly because it is an extreme scenario, and it is just a movie, but it speaks to an issue and a growing issue within our world, and it is that people are generally distrusting. Recently, I did a Google search on the word "trust," and I looked at the word through the various parts of speech, and I also went to look at the sample sentences as well. And when I got to seeing trust as a verb, I wanted to see how Google used to trust in action. And I found this interesting. Google defined the action of trust as:

believe in the reliability, truth, ability, or strength of.

And now, here is the sample sentence:

"I should have never trusted her."

Here is why I found this to be so interesting. Because Google, which I believe does everything with extreme intentionality, found it more applicable to use trust in action within a negative context rather than a positive one. I believe that says something about the current state of our society. It does not take long within our human experience to become distrustful. From the moment we are born, we are looking for things like: love, safety, and to be seen—a mentor of mine says it this way "You come out of the womb looking for someone looking for you," and the moment someone is unloving, or threatening—we begin to notice that maybe not all is well within the world. Maybe you are reading this book right now, and you are very much a skeptic across the board- there are a lot of industries in which people are highly skeptical within our world (politics, the school system, the healthcare system, the Church) and the majority of our society is polarized when it comes to these issues. We have been conditioned to not talk about two primary things: politics and religion, but now it is even expanding beyond those issues—we do not talk about our positions when it comes to medicine, vaccines, covid and other illnesses alike. And while everyone has their reasons for being skeptical about this or that, this book addresses people who may have allowed skepticism in with how they think about God. And before you think I'm demonizing skepticism, I am not—I believe theology must allow for mystery. But there are forms of skepticism that I believe to be unfounded and I am seeking to address those specific areas of skepticism in regard to God.

Maybe for you, the skepticism you have towards God is strictly around His existence, and you would hold to an agnostic or even an atheistic worldview. Which, I would say—I personally believe that the Christian worldview offers ample reason for belief. I have always preached that one of the greatest apologetics of the Christian faith is Christians (sadly, Christians can also be one the greatest hindrances of evangelism), but the reason why I would say that Christians themselves are such a great apologetic is because of life change. Within the church that I pastor, we have people who come from all different walks of life and have traveled so many various roads and yet we gather together as a community of people because of the life that we have found in Jesus because outside of that, there is not a whole lot of commonalities. When you think about it, most churches are just a Hodge podge of people who love Jesus. When I came into the church that I currently Pastor at, we held a "town hall" meeting if you will, and the point was so that the existing body would be able to get to know me and for me to get to know them and share the vision that I had for the church because we were going to be undergoing a church revitalization effort. I was twenty-six years old at that time. I stood up in a room where the majority of the hairs were grey. I do not say that as a negative thing, but that was just the reality of the situation. So that night, I said, "I'm serious about the lost people in our neighborhoods and around the world, and I want to see revival, and quite frankly, we are going to be changing a lot of things around here" (I still do not think that anyone was fully ready for all the things that were going to change, and I am little shocked that they went with that messaging). Still, nonetheless, I ended my talk with a time of question and answer—the first question I got was from a little old lady named Bonnie; Bonnie had been the church secretary for fifty-four years, and she had played the organ for close to seventy years, and she says to me: I have been coming to this church now for seventy-eight years, how do you at twenty-six years old expect to relate to me? Do you know what she was asking me without asking me? She wanted to know how she could trust me to be her pastor when it would be culturally so hard to relate to one another. And so, my response was—the Church seen in the new testament was really diverse, especially when you look at the church at Philippi, because when Paul went to Philippi in Acts 16- you see the church plant really began with diversity, there was: Lydia (a wealthy woman), a slave girl, and a prison guard- this is the launch team in which Paul forms, and then in Philippians chapter 1 Paul is remembering his time when he was first there in Philippi and then he gives this charge:

> Whatever happens, conduct yourselves in a manner worthy of the gospel of Christ. Then, whether I come and see you or only hear about you in my absence, I will know that you stand firm in the one Spirit, striving together as one for the faith of the gospel [28] without being frightened in any way by those who oppose you. This is a sign to them that they will be destroyed, but that you will be saved— and that by God. (Philippians 1:27-28)

Paul says, "striving together as one"... a picture of how the church should be unified and living on mission with one another even in the midst of so much diversity. So much so that Paul says that the world around you will not know what to do with you, that if you were that united, and so for one another, those who would oppose your message would know that they would not be able to tear you apart. And so, at the end of my response to Bonnie, I said, if the mission of God is what I want to see happen here, and it is what you want to do, and if we could unite on that front, I think we will be all right, and I know that the Enemy that the Church has will not like to see what goes on here. Bonnie very much appreciated that answer.

And so, when I preach on a Sunday morning, I look out at the congregation. I see people who, through love for Jesus, have experienced a life change, and this "life change" we refer to as testimonies. I truly believe that God wants to use testimonies. A testimony is not just a story to be told but a display of God's work to be seen. Testimonies are a powerful argument for the reality of

Jesus. So much so, that when the Apostle Paul went to Corinth, look what he says:

> And so it was with me, brothers and sisters. When I came to you, I did not come with eloquence or human wisdom as I proclaimed to you the testimony about God. ² For I resolved to know nothing while I was with you except Jesus Christ and him crucified. (I Corinthians 2:1-2)

When Paul showed up to Corinth, he said, I did not come to you, proclaiming to you the testimony of God with lofty wisdom or speech, but instead, I decided to know nothing among you except for Christ and Him Crucified. I love how Paul uses the words "For I resolved" or "I decided" because Paul was on a different intellectual level than almost anyone in his day, and quite frankly, throughout the history of the world, he was provided the best education, went to the greatest schools, and had the most seasoned mentors, and would have had no trouble presenting a Ted Talk on why the Christian faith made sense intellectually, but no he decided, he made a choice not to do that. And look at what his choice of knowing nothing but Christ and him crucified led him to:

> I came to you in weakness with great fear and trembling. ⁴ My message and my preaching were not with wise and persuasive words (I Corinthians 2:3-4a)

Paul came to Corinth with the evangelistic strategy that he had led him to come in weakness and with great fear and trembling. I wonder why Paul added that part to his letter? Why would he want his audience to know that he was afraid? Because our natural tendency is to rely on what we know, and yes, Paul knew about Christ and Him crucified, but he also knew a lot more than that- but he was not looking to show up and have a debate on various philosophies (though he very well could have done that). And I think as brilliant as Paul was, he would not be able to connect every dot for a skeptic because his wisdom and knowledge had a ceiling. If you are reading this book, and your skepticism is around the idea of God's existence, and the barrier to belief for you is that you need every dot to connect, I want to say this to you, if you are waiting for every dot to connect, you will die staring at dots. The finite mind will never fully be able to comprehend an infinite God. And because Paul understood the limitations of human wisdom—he blows the roof off and comes with something even more profound than any persuasive speech:

> but with a demonstration of the Spirit's power, [5] so
> that your faith might not rest on human wisdom,
> but on God's power. (I Corinthians 2:4b-5)

Do you know what Paul just said? He says, "Look at my life." I did not come to tell you a story that you could listen to and feel all warm and fuzzy inside, but instead, I came to allow you to see what God can do in someone's life. That tells me that a testimony is not just a story to be told but also a display of God's work to be seen. Because before, Paul was an Apostle and one of the greatest missionary and church planters the world has ever seen. Before all of that, he was a man named Saul of Tarsus. Saul hated the church—he mocked, beat, imprisoned, and killed followers of Jesus. And yet, look what happens right in the middle of it all:

> Meanwhile, Saul was still breathing out murderous
> threats against the Lord's disciples. He went to
> the high priest [2] and asked him for letters to the
> synagogues in Damascus so that if he found any
> there who belonged to the Way, whether men
> or women, he might take them as prisoners to
> Jerusalem.[3] As he neared Damascus on his journey,

suddenly a light from heaven flashed around him. [4] He fell to the ground and heard a voice say to him, "Saul, Saul, why do you persecute me?"

[5] "Who are you, Lord?" Saul asked.

"I am Jesus, whom you are persecuting," he replied. [6] "Now get up and go into the city, and you will be told what you must do." (Acts 9:1-6)

Like right in the middle, Saul of Tarsus goes after followers of Jesus, "still breathing out murderous threats" against them. It says that Saul went to go on a trip to Damascus because there he could gain a legal right to throw followers of Jesus into prison. This man is off the rails, and nothing is going to quench the anger that he has toward this movement of people. However, the story takes a turn while he is taking his horse to that old town road (I hope you caught that reference, if not, it's not for you), and on his way to Damascus, God knocks him off of his horse and blinds him and tells him, "knock it off Saul, no more of this persecution towards my people. In fact, you are going to start following me now." No one saw this coming. It would have been like Bin Laden saying, hey, I had this supernatural thing happen to me, and now I'm going to be preaching about the good news of Jesus. Talk about skepticism- there was a ton of skepticism surrounding Saul's conversion to Jesus. I want you to see the height of the skepticism. Check this out:

In Damascus there was a disciple named Ananias. The Lord called to him in a vision, "Ananias!"

"Yes, Lord," he answered.

[11] The Lord told him, "Go to the house of Judas on Straight Street and ask for a man from Tarsus

named Saul, for he is praying. [12] In a vision he has seen a man named Ananias come and place his hands on him to restore his sight."

[13] "Lord," Ananias answered, "I have heard many reports about this man and all the harm he has done to your holy people in Jerusalem. [14] And he has come here with authority from the chief priests to arrest all who call on your name." (Acts 9:10-14)

God tells Ananias, "Hey, that guy Saul from Tarsus, he's pretty close by. Would you mind swinging into the house he is at? I just need you to restore his eyesight." At this point, Ananias has not been clued in on the transformation that has occurred. Still, nonetheless, God, through a vision, is asking Ananias to go do something. Ananias begins to argue with the vision that he is having. How messed up did Saul of Tarsus have to be for Ananias to argue with a vision from God?

There were moments when Paul would look back on and think about that moment on that old Damascus Road. I wonder if he ever had to pinch himself to make sure he was not dreaming. Look at what he says to Timothy (his son in the faith):

I thank Christ Jesus our Lord, who has given me strength, that he considered me trustworthy, appointing me to his service. [13] Even though I was once a blasphemer and a persecutor and a violent man, I was shown mercy because I acted in ignorance and unbelief. [14] The grace of our Lord was poured out on me abundantly, along with the faith and love that are in Christ Jesus. [15] Here is a trustworthy saying that deserves full acceptance: Christ Jesus came into the world to save sinners—of whom I am the worst. [16] But for that very reason I

was shown mercy so that in me, the worst of sinners,
Christ Jesus might display his immense patience as
an example for those who would believe in him and
receive eternal life. (I Timothy 1:12-16)

When you look at Paul's resume before God called him to follow
him, Paul says there was nothing I could ever take credit for. My only
response is thankfulness because if I look at what I was bringing to
the table—it was nothing but baggage, and I gave God every reason
not to choose me. And yet, God allowed me to live the life I did
so that He might show the rest of the world just how patient and
merciful He is.

There are times when Paul talks about his former life, and
he mentions the accolades that he acquired in his pursuit of
self-righteousness:

If someone else thinks they have reasons to put
confidence in the flesh, I have more: [5] circumcised
on the eighth day of the people of Israel, of the
tribe of Benjamin, a Hebrew of Hebrews; in regard
to the law, a Pharisee; [6] as for zeal, persecuting
the church; as for righteousness based on the law,
faultless (Philippians 3:4-6)

Paul says I had the trophy rooms of trophy rooms, no one could
touch the records that I was breaking…and he would later call it all
garbage (v.8). But when you see Paul looking back on his testimony
in I Timothy, he also says that there was another accolade that he
gained in his former life—he says I was the chief of sinners (1:15).
Paul was acknowledging that even in the midst of his self-righteous
pursuit, that there wasn't a greater sinner than he.

And so, to go from being the chief of sinners and a violent
opponent of God to becoming a man who was willing to die for the
faith that he was once trying to destroy, how does this happen? This

is what Paul's argument in Corinth is, it is "look at my life! How do you explain this?" And so, Paul coming to a group of people, determined the greatest argument that he could make was not his mind but his life. And he points to the Holy Spirit and says that is the only explanation that could make sense of what happened to me on that road.

If the skepticism, you have regarding God is based on His existence—I'd point to the reality of the change that God makes in the lives of so many people. And you do not even need to stop there. There are so many more points to consider regarding God's existence: the evidence that surrounds Jesus's resurrection, the accuracy of the biblical manuscripts, the fact that the Bible was written over the course of 1500 years, by 40 different authors, in multiple languages, and on multiple continents and yet all of the writing points to the same one big idea: God. From Genesis to Revelation, the Bible is about God and His revelation to mankind. You could look at the visible world around us and point to the fact that we have an intelligent design, and if you have an intelligent design, then you have an intelligent designer. In a world of varying philosophies and thoughts on origin theory and deities, the monsoon amount of evidence pointing to the triune God of the Bible cannot be ignored. There is so much more I would like to write on the existence of God—but for now, I want to address skepticism in regard to God's character. The title of this book is 26 letters but stuck on y, as in, for most people, the problem of pain is a dilemma, and it leads to wonder and/or confusion. When C.S. Lewis wrote his book "The Problem of Pain," he commented that he did not even want to write on this subject. We are regularly reminded of the fallenness, yet dealing with hardships has not gotten any easier. And so, when I think about the idea of skepticism regarding God's character, I think of the book of Job.

The book starts with a man named Job, and Job so desired to please God that it says that he literally "shunned evil" (Job 1:1) and then furthermore, it goes on to say that not only is Job rich in the sense that he loves God and hates sin but that he also has a great amount of financial wealth. And so, that is the context for how the book begins. Then it does a turn and begins a new plot, almost like a Quinton Tarantino movie, where multiple plots are going on at once. Yet, separately but also intertwined…yeah, that is what's happening. The new scene is now of Satan and God having a dialogue—in which satan appears in God's presence and ultimately says that he was roaming the earth, and that is all Satan says. Yet, God says, "Did you by chance get a glimpse of Job?" "He is pretty amazing, isn't he?…his love for me is undeniable." Why did God bring up Job? Satan didn't bring him up although the fact that Satan knew of Job's wealth (Job 1:10) tells me that Satan did know Job.

And it is interesting what assumption Satan makes:

> "Have you not put a hedge around him, his household, and everything he has? You have blessed the work of his hands so that his flocks and herds are spread throughout the land. (Job 1:10)

Satan says, "of course he loves you. You have given him everything that he could ever want." Often times we think that prosperity equates to blessing and that desolation equates to punishment. And that if we were to have a lot, then it would be easier to worship, and honestly, it is a trap of Satan to get us to believe that because what happens more often than not—prosperity will lead humanity away from God (disclaimer: prosperity does not always lead humanity away from God and nor is wealth evil in and of itself) and maybe you feel uneasy with that statement, or you do not agree with what I wrote, and so if that is you, let me challenge you to do an in-depth study throughout the old testament of how well Israel does with prosperity. They never handle it well—it always leads to rebellion, to the worship of idols. The book of Hosea is a real-life illustration between the prophet Hosea and his wife Gomer, who is a prostitute. This relationship illustrated God's love for Israel (now Hosea and

Gomer were real people), but ultimately it was a way for God to give a tangible illustration that God's people might understand the depth of His love). And look at what God says about his Love for Israel and how they handled blessing:

> "When Israel was a child, I loved him,
> and out of Egypt I called my son.
> ² But the more they were called,
> the more they went away from me.
> They sacrificed to the Baals
> and they burned incense to images. (Hosea 11:1-2)

God said, "The more I loved Israel, the more they turned away from me." And so, in this situation with Job, Satan says he does not love you. He just loves your stuff. That is not always a fair thing to say because historically, as seen by God in Hosea, blessing often leads to rebellion. It appears that Job's love for God is legitimate. God says to Satan, if you think it is the stuff he loves, I'll allow you to take it away. The condition is that you do not harm Job. So, in one day—Job has everything stripped from him, and he loses all his family (minus his wife) as Job goes on, she is not encouraging at all to him and attempts to lead Job away from God. Not only does Job lose his kids, but he also loses all his cattle- which that was the commerce of the day. Livestock drove the economy, and it was like his bank and retirement accounts all got drained the same day. I have definitely had some bad days, and I'm sure you have days and weeks that you have tried to block out of your memory because of how difficult they were, but this is a story that is hard to one up. And yet, despite losing everything, Job does not turn his back on God. Look at his response to the loss of everything he had:

> ²⁰ At this, Job got up and tore his robe and shaved
> his head. Then he fell to the ground in worship ²¹
> and said:

"Naked I came from my mother's womb,
and naked I will depart.
The Lord gave and the Lord has taken away;
may the name of the Lord be praised."
²² In all this, Job did not sin by charging God with
wrongdoing. (Job 1:20-22)

Job got up and tore his robe and shaved his head (this was a sign that he was mourning), and what happens next is beautiful because it says that "he fell to the ground in worship," which says to me that worshipping and mourning do not have to be mutually exclusive— worship and mourning can be seated at the same table, and mourning does not diminish the value of the worship. If anything, it may increase the value of the worship. And though God permitted Satan to take away Job's world as he knew it, look at what Job said within his worship. Look whom he credits the loss of all his things too— God! But wait? Wasn't it Satan? Job here is acknowledging God's sovereignty and that nothing happens apart from God's control. This concept is so hard to come to terms with because it does not assume that God is the active agent giving out suffering, but it does show us that He knows it is coming and has the ability to stop it. I do not personally believe that God gave me Crohn's Disease, but I do believe that He saw it coming for me and, within His plan, did not see it best to stop it. I wish I could say that I was like Job and could instantaneously begin to worship God—it took me years to be able to look back on that two-month visit in the hospital and see that it was a time when God was loving me, and moving and preparing me for the life He was leading me into. I have often said that that was the best two months and worst two months of my life, and I would never want to relive that experience, but I would not want to miss out on all that God did. And this point is not meant to serve as some cheap hope that cannot bear the weight of your suffering. I understand it could be years, or decades, or possibly never on this side of eternity that you feel like you had a good understanding of why you endured what you did, past or present.

And though Job was able to praise God during loss, the people around him could not understand—in the eyes of Job's wife and friends, he had every reason to leave God high and dry. And the suffering intensified because Satan went back to God and God says, hey, you said that if Job lost it all he would lose his worship of me, and that did not happen, to which Satan replies and says yeah, but if his physical health was attacked, that would be the icing on top of the cake, there is no way that Job maintains his worship of you if he lost his health too. The former prohibition of Satan was that he did not harm Job, and that gets loosened up to now. It is that Satan is not to kill Job (2:6) and so Satan plagues Job's body with painful boils from his head to his feet. This is just a really sad picture, a guy who lost everything that meant something to him (besides his wife) and is now experiencing major physical turmoil, to the point that in order to get any sense of relief, look at what he does:

> [7] So Satan went out from the presence of the Lord
> and afflicted Job with painful sores from the soles
> of his feet to the crown of his head. [8] Then Job took
> a piece of broken pottery and scraped himself with
> it as he sat among the ashes. (Job 2:7-8)

Job's wife comes up and says, "When are you going to curse God and die you fool?" (Job 2:9) Now, I am newly married, but I could imagine the necessity for you and your spouse to be on the same page when going through this kind of conflict. And what you can gather from Job's wife's comment is that she is not encouraging him to grow deeper with the Lord. She is attempting to create doubt in the character of God, that if God is giving you difficulty, then He must not be worthy of worship. Job does not get defensive. He does not say, "Why did you call me a fool??" Rather, Job takes the opportunity to remind her of his belief about God:

He replied, "You are talking like a foolish woman.
Shall we accept good from God, and not trouble?"
(Job 2:10)

Job essentially just said to his wife that her theology is misunderstood and that God allows both good and bad to befall our lives. The reality that God allows both good and bad to befall our lives is a beautiful truth and should offer comfort (I will explain shortly). And yet, I am sure most of us have had very well-meaning, loving family and friends attempt to encourage us, that whatever hardship we are or were going through, God was absent from the equation. Here is why I said that it is really a beautiful thing that God allows both the good and the bad to befall our lives because if the statement is that God is absent from our suffering, then that absence would communicate to me a lack of care. I mean, think about that for a second, so many people have deep wounds from parents or family members who were absent from their lives. I have sat and counseled people who were so driven in their careers that it was to the neglect of family, and there are always wounds that accompany that lifestyle. Yet, we think that saying God is absent somehow bolsters some level of confidence in God's goodness. In the New Testament, Jesus would reinforce that God is present amidst the suffering:

> [29] Are not two sparrows sold for a penny? Yet not one
> of them will fall to the ground outside your Father's
> care. [30] And even the very hairs of your head are all
> numbered. [31] So don't be afraid; you are worth more
> than many sparrows. (Matthew 10:29-31)

Jesus says that there is not something so insignificant that is happening in the world where God is not deeply interested. Jesus says: if you had any doubt on whether God the Father cares about the things you are going through, then look at the sparrows, they are worth nothing, and He has not gotten too preoccupied with other things to not still know and stay involved. You have every reason to believe that if God so cares for the sparrows in their time of trouble, then He has not forgotten about you.

> "Child of God, you cost Christ too much for him
> to forget you." Charles Spurgeon

And not only is God's allowance for trouble to befall our lives a comfort in the fact that God cares, but it is also a comfort in the fact that if God is not present within our suffering, then we should have no certainty that good could come from our pain. How does God make all things beautiful in their time (Ecclesiastes 3:11) if He is not present when life is ugly? God has, throughout human history, love to take what Satan means for evil and turn it back around on Satan. Look at the life of the Apostle Paul, he had a past and God used his past to platform his future. The only way God is looking to rid you of your past hurts is by using them to build your future. And if He is not present amidst the pain, you have no hope that your pain ever gets used for good. Tim Challies wrote:

> If God is not sovereign, you are not secure (Tim
> Challies; If God is not sovereign, article)

So, in essence, Job looked at his wife and told her, "Do not rob me of the hope that God is in control." And you would think that what Job knew would be evidenced in the way he went about his life. What Job knew he did not know. Do you know what I mean by that? I could tell you all about how beautiful the smokey mountains are, but unless you go and experience them, you do not really know. Job was able to spout off ideas about God—but Job did not truly grasp the magnitude of God. Because as the book goes on, you see these various dialogues that Job has with his motley crew of friends, and within those conversations, you see that Job makes points about not understanding how God would allow this to happen to someone who was so righteous. And in a way, Job was making the accusation that God was allowing this series of losses to come to the wrong guy. However, Job did have one friend who came in and rebuked Job and the three musketeers:

> So these three men stopped answering Job, because he was righteous in his own eyes. [2] But Elihu, son of Barakel the Buzite, of the family of Ram, became very angry with Job for justifying himself rather than God. [3] He was also angry with the three friends, because they had found no way to refute Job and yet had condemned him. [4] Now Elihu had waited before speaking to Job because they were older than he. [5] But when he saw that the three men had nothing more to say, his anger was aroused. (Job 32:1-5)

And for six chapters- Elihu goes on to remind Job that his righteousness pales in comparison to God. And following Elihu's rebuke, God the Father responds to Job's accusation (why is God allowing bad things to happen to someone as good as me?) and reminds Job of who He is. The longest discourse of God the Father in the entirety of the scriptures is found in Job 38-41, and in that discourse you would think that maybe He answers Job's why—you would think maybe He offers Job comfort by explaining the why behind losing his children, and his wealth. But no, that is not what God does. God offers comfort by reminding Job about who He is (His character and nature).

In a day and age where we get to have answers on demand, it can be difficult for us to sit and not know. I'm sure all of us would love for God to connect the dots for us, for every why question that we would ever have, and at the end of the day, do you know what that would do for you? —Those answers would settle your curiosity but not necessarily provide you comfort. Job never was told his "why." He was given a bigger and clearer picture of the Who he was asking his "why" to. And it is the knowledge of God's character and nature that provided comfort. When we think of whether God can be trusted, it is more of a question of God's character than anything else. Yet- we think that our ability to trust is whether or not we know the "why." Knowledge provides clarity, while true knowledge of God's character and nature provides comfort.

If you are in the midst of your "'why" and are doubting whether or not God can be trusted, let me share with you the words of the Apostle Paul in Romans 8:

> [32] He who did not spare his own Son, but gave him up for us all—how will he not also, along with him, graciously give us all things? (Romans 8:32)

If you need any level of confidence in God's care for your pain— look to the cross of Jesus Christ. The cross is evidence that God cares for you. When the good creation fell away from grace and God's presence and the world was plagued by sin—God did not look at His creation and say I no longer care about communion with my people—but God entered into the brokenness by sending His Son Jesus into the world to offer salvation. While absence would be evidence for lack of care, presence would demonstrate a level of care. You do not get involved with the things you do not care about.

> For God so loved the world that he gave his one and only Son, that whoever believes in him shall not perish but have eternal life. (John 3:16)

God cares.

CHAPTER 2

WILL THIS LAST FOREVER?

> One of the greatest strains in life is the strain of
> waiting for God.- Oswald Chambers

Amidst your suffering, some of the questions you may be asking are...how much longer? When will this end? I think those questions are naturally tied to pain of any kind. Most of us, if we were to have any kind of surgery, or procedure done, we would always want to know- how long is the recovery? When will I begin to feel back to normal? And the longer the duration of our suffering, the more apt our mind is to build a case or narrative to believe that this is our forever reality or that there is no end in sight. You may be sitting here reading and the suffering you have endured has been decades in the making, and the last thing I want to do is give you some sense of false hope as if reading this book is the cure-all to the pain you are feeling. My guess would be that I have not the slightest clue of what you are feeling or what you have been through, nor do I want to pretend. I want to do my best to not make blanket statements. But I do relate to the feeling of "How much longer?" For you, you may not be viewing your situation as suffering, but maybe it is just an angst you feel in your soul because you are waiting...waiting for that job, waiting for that special someone to come into your life, waiting for your spouse to step up and show you love and meet your needs, waiting for a wayward child to return home, waiting for the stock market to fly through the roof. The human experience goes hand in hand with waiting. And that is hard to reconcile with the fact that we live in the age of smart technology, which means we do not like waiting for anything, we want answers on demand (thank you, Google), we want instant gratification (thank your social media), we want our hunger to be met in an instance (insert your favorite fast food, guilty pleasure stop here). In the metro Detroit area, I regularly drive past places with big signs that say, "Cash your check TODAY." Most digital platforms of exchanging money (Cash App and Venmo) exist and make money because they take a fee to transfer money instantly into your bank as opposed to waiting 2-3 days for it to settle in your bank. This is the fast-paced world we live in, and yet within the school of affliction, many of the classrooms seem to go way past the ring of the bell. Do you follow that thought? Days of hardships are the only days that we get that last longer than twenty-four hours. The days of difficulty are not like any other. And so, we are met with these "why" questions because we do not know how to reconcile God's timing with our circumstances, because if God was truly good, and He was all-powerful, why on earth would he allow the circumstances that we face to endure for the duration that they do?

I myself am no foreigner to pain and suffering. I can think of moments in my life when the thought of getting better seemed like a distant fairytale in a far-off land. If I can be totally honest with you- the doubts were real- I began wondering if there could really be a God because if He was real, was He just not aware of the circumstances that I was enduring? Did He know and just not care? If that was the case, then, He certainly was not good, nor was He worthy of my worship. And the longer my suffering went on for, the more that doubt grew.

My own story of pain and suffering stems back to 2011. I was seventeen years old at the time and I was just diagnosed with Crohn's Disease, and I had a hard time reconciling that diagnosis as a teenager. Because my thought at that moment in time as these are the years that are supposed to be full of life and free of pain, and the time when nothing bad happens. Hindsight is such a clear 20/20, and I wish that what I know now is what I knew then because I do not claim to be an expert on much. If I'm honest, I know a little bit about a little bit, but one thing I know for certain is: pain comes. I have yet to meet a person who has a life story in which pain was absent. Maybe for you, it was a parent who was abusive (physically, emotionally, spiritually) or you got involved in a relationship where you were treated cheaply. Maybe you were a victim of bullying in some fashion, or you endured financial hardships, or your mind and heart have been riddled with depression and anxiety, or you have undergone a physical medical diagnosis. My guess is within that short list, there is something that pertains to the bulk of humanity to which they would relate.

And because these are realities of the human experience, and because we live in such a fast-paced world, what do we do when we are praying for circumstances to change and they do not? That's typically when the pit in our soul begins to feel sour, and the doubts creep into our mind that if God is real, how could He ever be trusted? Certainly, He could fix or end the misery that we are enduring.

I am sure many of us can relate to the prophet Habakkuk. Although Habakkuk was a prophet, he was not a typical prophet because a prophet in the Old Testament was one who would speak to the people on God's behalf, but at no point in the book of Habakkuk do you see him do that. He never once addresses the people, but rather, he talks to God on behalf of the people. Habakkuk lives in a moment in history where when he looks around, and here's what he sees: he says the righteous (God's people) are suffering, and then he says that the wicked (Assyrian and Babylonian empires) are prospering. Oftentimes in the midst of struggling, it is easy to look at the prettiness of everybody else's life. We can even do a game of measuring, where we would say or think things like: why is that happening to me and not my _____ (fill in the blank) because that person, they do x,y, and z and their life seems to be going great, why is their marriage seemingly going so good? Why don't they have financial struggles? Why is their health appearing to be well? None of us would ever want to verbalize those thoughts, but I am sure, at times, they have crept in.

I can recall in 2014. This was shortly after the Lord made it clear to me that I would give my time and energy to pastoral ministry that I had undergone a terrible surgery that had me in a nearby hospital for nearly two months. None of that seemed fair to me. There was complication after complication, and the light at the end of the tunnel was dim. I could remember looking at social media, and seeing people that were the weekend warrior, partying it up and living far from God, and wondering why does something like this happen to me? Like, I viewed my life as a blank signed check to God and said I'll go where you want me to go, and I'll do what you want me to do, and it seemed like the hospital was an odd place to end up for someone who had that heartbeat. Shouldn't bad things be reserved for bad people? That's an assumption that causes a lot of people to not understand grace. And it's an assumption that leads people to have a misunderstanding of suffering. I like what one pastor/author said pertaining to this idea:

> Comfort is the god of our generation, so suffering is
> seen as a problem to be solved, and not a providence
> from God. (Matt Chandler; Cross 2013)

We oftentimes look at suffering as a punishment, and that's probably because there are natural consequences to certain behaviors (like when we see that there are medical diagnosis's linked to obesity, alcoholism, sex, etc.), and so, our mind can do the same thing with sin. It's not a far stretch for us to think the severity of sin should equate to the severity of suffering. In fact, Jesus actually rebuked this teaching in John 9 with the man who was born blind. The disciples of Jesus asked Jesus, was this man born blind because he sinned or because his parents sinned? Jesus says, "Neither" Jesus debunked the idea that hardships are always a result of sin, but rather this was a result of the display of God's working. And that's the beauty about God, that He is at work even when we do not see His working nor understand His plan.

And so, when Habakkuk looks at the problem of evil in the world, his question is, God where are you? How much longer are you going to let this go on?

> O Lord, how long shall I cry for help,
> and you will not hear?
> Or cry to you "Violence!"
> and you will not save?
> ³ Why do you make me see iniquity,
> and why do you idly look at wrong?
> Destruction and violence are before me;
> strife and contention arise.
> ⁴ So the law is paralyzed,
> and justice never goes forth.
> For the wicked surround the righteous;
> so justice goes forth perverted. (Habakkuk 1:2-4)

Habakkuk cannot fathom how God can allow the wicked to have the seemingly upper hand "for the wicked surround the righteous," and because this is the present reality for Habakkuk, he's left with the question "How long shall I cry for help," or cry to you "VIOLENCE" Habakkuk says I've done anything and everything to get your attention, and still, all I hear is crickets. Likewise, for people like you and me, we have a whole slew of attempts to gain God's attention: if I just read my bible more, if I just pray more, if I just volunteer more, then maybe I will unlock some code that gains God's attention. And that kind of behavior really shows us our view of God, and that view is not that He is a Sovereign ruler of both Heaven and Earth, but it is that He is a genie in a bottle that I send my wish list to. Please do not take that last comment to mean that we cannot pray to God about all things, I do not prescribe to that idea, but if our obedience is strictly predicated on the hopes of circumstances going our way, then we do not have a proper understanding of God and how He works. Because sometimes, we can plead for God to give us something that is not good, and receiving the answer "no" can be an unseen grace. Because God is accomplishing something. And that is what God tells the prophet Habakkuk, he says I see, I understand, I hear you, you guys are going through difficult times, and so, don't worry, I will make provision for you:

> "Look among the nations, and see;
> wonder and be astounded.
> For I am doing a work in your days
> that you would not believe if told.
> ⁶ For behold, I am raising up the Chaldeans,
> that bitter and hasty nation,
> who march through the breadth of the earth,
> to seize dwellings not their own.
> ⁷ They are dreaded and fearsome;
> their justice and dignity go forth from themselves.
> ⁸ Their horses are swifter than leopards,
> more fierce than the evening wolves;
> their horsemen press proudly on.
> Their horsemen come from afar;
> they fly like an eagle swift to devour.
> ⁹ They all come for violence,
> all their faces forward.
> They gather captives like sand.
> ¹⁰ At kings they scoff,
> and at rulers they laugh.
> They laugh at every fortress,
> for they pile up earth and take it.

¹¹ Then they sweep by like the wind and go on,
guilty men, whose own might is their god!"
(Habakkuk 1:5-11)

What a response from God. It starts off sounding amazing, doesn't it? He says, man Habakkuk, if you only knew what I was doing, and even if you were told, I promise you, wouldn't believe it because of how awesome this plan is. The beauty of that build-up is that God is going to tell Habakkuk his plan in response to Habakkuk's plea/question. Now remember, Habakkuk says, "God, we (your people) need your help because Assyria is an evil people and we are being oppressed by them." Do you know what God says in response to this? He says, "Ok Habakkuk, I will take your Assyria and raise you a Babylon," essentially, what God just said to Habakkuk is, my plan is to take out the Assyrian empire with Babylon. They are much bigger, stronger, and more violent and treacherous people. Probably not what Habakkuk was looking for. Oftentimes in our crying out to God, we have a very intended hopeful outcome to our prayers- and the question we must wrestle with is, do we trust God when His answers do not align with our hopes and dreams? Will we be tempted to make more accusations against God? Habakkuk says in response to that- God, I thought you were good? How is this your solution? Babylon? Really? And ultimately, what God was doing, He was teaching His people about His faithfulness because, ultimately, the promise was going to be to remove Babylon, seen in the bulk of chapter two, woe to any enemy of God. And so, a lesson within the book of Habakkuk is no matter how bleak, or difficult or dark the circumstance that you may be faced with, that God will be faithful. Now again, that does not mean that God's faithfulness always grants us everything that we could ever want, but it means that God's plans are always good. That means when life's circumstances are not fair or tempting you to believe that God cannot be trusted, that is not the time to run but to embrace. Ironically enough, that is what the name Habakkuk means. It means to embrace or to wrestle with. God is not afraid of the doubts that creep into your heart and mind, and one of the worst things you can do is try to pretend that those doubts do not exist. You will miss the intimacy of being with God in your weakness. There is a beauty afforded to the struggler that you do not get to experience in the mountaintops of life. So do not waste your hurt or miss that moment with God. There are so many moments in scripture where you see this reality lived out. In one of the most famous Psalms, Psalm 23, David begins the Psalm by speaking about God, that God is a good shepherd and David shares about various attributes of God's shepherding that have afforded him peace. Then there is a transition in the Psalm where David goes from speaking about God to David speaking to God. It is really beautiful. Here is what he says when he begins speaking to God:

> Even though I walk through the valley of the
> shadow of death,
> I will fear no evil,
> for you are with me;
> your rod and your staff,
> they comfort me.
> ⁵ You prepare a table before me
> in the presence of my enemies;
> you anoint my head with oil;
> my cup overflows.
> ⁶ Surely goodness and mercy shall follow me
> all the days of my life,
> and I shall dwell in the house of the Lord
> forever. (Psalm 23:4-6)

David says, when I am in the thick of it, when darkness is all around me, to the point where he says, "I am in the shadow of death." When those days come and that loved one is nearing the end, when the days come of financial crisis, when the days come and the doctor calls, when the days come, and they do, and they will, David says, "I'll fear no evil." How? How is this possible—"for you are with me." Sheep are never closer to the shepherd than when they are in a valley. Even the Apostle Paul spoke to this truth that we experience a deep intimacy with God in II Corinthians 12 when he shares how God's power is made perfect in weakness (verse 9) and because of that reality, Paul says I'll boast all the more gladly about my weaknesses so that the power of Christ may rest upon me (verse 9). Paul acknowledges that there is a unique opportunity of experiencing Christ's power that is felt in weakness—throughout Paul's theology Paul never tries to deny the reality of hardships:

> We are afflicted in every way, but not crushed; perplexed, but not driven to despair; ⁹ persecuted, but not forsaken; struck down, but not destroyed (II Corinthians 4:8-9)

Afflicted in every way. People who love God can still experience suffering in any and all kinds of ways. No one reading this book is immune to receiving a phone call or text at this very moment that could ruin your day, weeks, months, and years. But Paul says though we feel all and every kind of pain, and we do not ever deny that reality, we are not crushed. In a moment, Paul will share in the passage why the pain (though very real) is not crushing. And it is what Paul says next that answers the question for me: will this last forever? Much of this chapter has dealt with the reality that pain comes. It is the undeniable reality of the human experience, and these experiences tend to last longer than any of our timetables would have ever hoped. And so, if this is where you are at, or this is where you have been, or if this is where you are going to be, and the question that seems at the height of your mind "will this last forever?" My answer is: I hope so. Maybe it is not the answer you were hoping for? Sorry, it is too late to get a refund. But I actually hope that the answer "I hope so" offers you a level of hope and encouragement. Because look at what Paul says for the reason he is not crushed:

> So we do not lose heart. Though our outer self is wasting away, our inner self is being renewed day by day. [17] For this light momentary affliction is preparing for us an eternal weight of glory beyond all comparison, [18] as we look not to the things that are seen but to the things that are unseen. For the things that are seen are transient, but the things that are unseen are eternal. (II Corinthians 4:16-18)

The reason behind not losing heart, even amidst the most difficult and trying times—Paul says it is because there is something else going on amidst the pain. Paul says that the inner self is being renewed, that God is doing things beyond what you can see in the midst of pain, and it is not temporary—it is eternal. What Paul says next requires careful consideration. He says, "For this light and momentary affliction"—I am confident that the hardships you have endured would not be best described as "light" or "momentary." For me, when I think about my two months in the hospital, nothing about that experience felt light or momentary. So, if the verse stopped there, I could not trust Paul, but thankfully that is not where the verse ends. Paul says, "This light and momentary affliction pales in comparison to the eternal weight of glory." Paul draws out the contrast. It is not that cancer is light or momentary, or the loss of loved ones is light and momentary, or financial hardship is light and momentary. It is that any ounce of suffering does not compare to the eternal weight of glory that suffering is producing. Because sometimes, people waste their suffering, but God never wastes suffering. I like what Joni Eareckson Tada wrote:

> "Sometimes God allows what he hates to accomplish what he loves." (Joni Eareckson Tada; The God I love)

Suffering and pain are not meaningless. And our inability to acknowledge a reason does not denote that there is one. When I was nineteen years old, and I was so confused and struggling with doubt and saw no more purpose in life because of the pain I was enduring, had you come and told me that I had no need to worry because there is a purpose to all this, I would not have been able to in my limited imagination been able to fathom any good reason for the suffering I was enduring? But fast-forward a decade later, and I see all the things now that God was accomplishing through my pain. Crohn's disease has been able to give me a platform to speak into people's lives. I have had countless calls with people going through medical issues and struggling with doubts and fears. I was able to relate to a group of people on a mission trip. I have seen pain become a platform, and because pain and suffering are universal to the human experience, pain often serves as a megaphone to the world around you. People listen to people who have been hurt. Hurt translates across space, time, and cultures.

Paul's rationale for not being crushed by any and all hardships is that there are eternal purposes tied to pain and suffering. And so, he says we look to the things that are unseen, "For the things that are seen are transient, but the things that are unseen are eternal." When you think about that verse, Paul talks about looking at the things that are unseen. In essence, Paul is petitioning us to give our energy and attention to what is God accomplishing through this pain or hardship that I am going through whether we see it or not. I love what one Pastor/author once tweeted out (see, Twitter can serve good purposes), John Piper:

"God is always doing ten thousand things in your life, and you may be aware of three of them" (John Piper; Desiring God Twitter). Friend, I, from the beginning, have not tried to pretend to know your story or your hurt and pain—but even if you described the full story to me—I would, in turn, tell you that I do not pretend to know all the ways that God is going to use your pain. If I am honest with you, I can recall sharing my story of pain in a sermon one time, and I said what I did not know at nineteen has now come full circle for me, and I understand. I see the purpose within the pain, and I had a friend come up to me shortly thereafter and lovingly said: "I do not think that the story of your pain has come full circle. I think that there is even more to the story still to be told." I absolutely believe that to be true. This book could even be evidence of that claim because it is the continuation of how God has continued to use my own story. So, is the difficulty you are going through going to last forever? I hope so. My prayer is that your suffering and hardships would serve you and others around you for much more than this lifetime here on earth.

CHAPTER 3

WHY CAN'T I SHAKE
THESE FEELINGS?

Many falsely suppose that the feelings, which God has implanted in
us as natural, proceed only from a defect. Accordingly, the perfecting
of believers does not depend on their casting off all feelings, but on
their yielding to them and controlling them, only for proper reason.

Within this chapter, I would like to lead with a disclaimer. I
understand that feelings of Anxiety and Depression can vary in
their root of origin from reasons that are either: Physical, Mental,
Emotional, or Spiritual. However, I will write about feelings from a
spiritual/theological perspective.

Feelings can be a really difficult thing to talk about. We all
have them, but very few of us know what to do with them. Partially
why feelings can be so difficult to talk about is because we hardly
understand them. I hope you are not feeling insulted, but my guess
would be that you are a work in progress. Otherwise, you would
be someone who never loses your cool. You have no conflicts in the
places where you live, work, and play. Chances are, you are like me,
and feelings can be tough. Our upbringing has a lot to do with how
we understand our feelings. Young boys often look to their dads as
a picture of how to handle their feelings; likewise, young girls will
take their cues from their moms. Maybe for you, you learned to

stuff them way down inside because that is what you saw, or you saw a parent become very expressive with their feelings and how they projected them are now the ways you imitate your demonstration of feelings. I have been part of Christian circles that have treated feelings as something to be ignored or that there is no place for feelings, I certainly do not land there, and on the flip side, I have seen groups of Christians treat their feelings like they held the same authority as God Himself. We have to be careful not to fall into either one of those extreme camps.

My first summer out of High School, a group of friends and myself were on our way to a kayaking/camping trip in Northern Michigan. I was ecstatic about the trip, to the point where I could not sleep the night before (like a kid on Christmas). I ended up pulling an all-nighter- and we were leaving at 5 am. We piled into two cars and were on our way. I was one of the drivers for our trip, and we were making our way up beautiful I-75 Northbound and we were making a great time. The roads were clear. About an hour into the drive, my friend (the other driver) decided to pull up next to me on the road, and he kept looking over at me, and then he threw me a head nod and gunned it. Naturally, to not be outdone, I floored it. We both got our cars up to going 100mph+. Now, the race was pretty short-lived because my friend (or at least the others in that car) decided this needed to stop, so they slowed down. I, on the other hand, was loving the timing we were making and so I just slowed down a wee bit. And as we were cruising along, I began to look at printed-out MapQuest directions (who remembers those days?) when a friend in the backseat encouraged me to put both hands back on the wheel. At that moment, I-75 was curving and we had just gone over the warning track and were inches away from the median wall. So, I jerked the wheel, crossed all four traffic lanes and began fishtailing. I could not control the vehicle, everyone in the car was screaming for their life, and I eventually slammed on the brakes. There was no reason that car should not have flipped. It had gotten to be that time in the morning when people were heading to work, and so how we did not slam into another vehicle was a complete act of God. We all determined it would be best to pull off on the next exit and regroup. To this day, I do not know of a time that I was ever more shaken up. I remember sitting on a curb at a gas station and having the thought of each of our parents receiving a death notification, and I realized how fortunate we were not to have died. A friend of mine from the other vehicle chewed me out pretty well. I would say she was justified in how she felt, but that surely was not helping how I felt. For me, the entirety of that trip was ruined. I could not shake the feeling that I had felt. I felt horrible, as if every muscle in my body was being quenched.

In most cases, seasons of hardships and difficulty can give way to all kinds of feelings, even warranted feelings and even some unwarranted feelings. Nonetheless, what are we to do when the feelings we have are not the feelings we want but cannot seem to shake the heartache?

There is this story in the Bible about these friends of Jesus who experience great loss, and they feel a particular way about it. It causes them frustration and hurt from Jesus, and yet Jesus meets them in their feelings and does not dismiss their feelings but instead helps to inform their feelings. It is the story of Mary, Martha, and Lazarus. It is found in John chapter 11. Here is how the story begins:

> Now a man named Lazarus was sick. He was from Bethany, the village of Mary and her sister Martha. [2] (This Mary, whose brother Lazarus now lay sick, was the same one who poured perfume on the Lord and wiped his feet with her hair.) [3] So the sisters sent word to Jesus, "Lord, the one you love is sick." (John 11:1-3)

Throughout the gospel accounts, you see much of Jesus's public ministry, but you just get little pockets of His personal life, and though it speaks little to Jesus's personal life, we do know that He had one and that these people were in it, evidenced by the fact, that the word that needs to get to Jesus is that "the one He loved was sick." Mary and Martha are in a position of watching their brother, Jesus's friend dying. Have you ever been around someone nearing the end? My guess would be that if you had, then that moment is probably burned into your memory. I can think of loved ones I have watched on their last day(s), and it is gut-wrenching when they look to be fighting for their next breath. That is where these sisters are at in this moment, and in heart of desperation, they knew that if Jesus could get here, then their brother was going to be ok. Words get to Jesus, and I am sure that if you heard one of your loved ones was nearing death, you would be dropping anything and everything to make sure you got to say your goodbyes. Now I want you to imagine that you are God in the flesh. You are not looking to rush there to say your goodbyes. Rather, you are looking to get there to save the day, to heal your friend. Which makes Jesus's response to the news all the more interesting:

> So when he heard that Lazarus was sick, he stayed
> where he was two more days, ⁷ and then he said to
> his disciples, "Let us go back to Judea." (John 11:6-7)

How cruel of a response? Right? Like, "Hey Jesus, urgent, emergency, 911, Lazarus is dying, please come help"…and the response to the news is that he looks at His disciples and says, "Let's wait here a couple of days."

I have been there. I have been in the place of feeling as though God was letting me down. I can remember those cold, dark nights in the hospital, and it was just me and God, thinking where are you and being overwhelmed by the feeling that I was alone in this. Chances are, if your suffering had any significant duration or urgency, you too, have felt these things.

The result of Jesus's waiting is that Lazarus died. The clock struck midnight, and Jesus was nowhere to be found. Now I believe that Jesus had a reason for the waiting, and the waiting fit within His plan—but from every earthly perspective, the ball was dropped. We oftentimes can feel as though Jesus shows up late to our situations, and yet over and over in the scriptures, God reveals that His timing is perfect, and calls us to things like: waiting, and patience, to slow down, and to trust Him in the interim (Isaiah 60:22; Habakkuk 2:3; Psalm 27:14). And while we have these instructions all throughout the breadth of scripture to wait, trust, and be patient—all of which are foreign to the nature of humanity. To respond with trust and patience amidst the waiting is not normal. Here is what is normal. Look what happens when Jesus shows up late to the home of Lazarus:

> On his arrival, Jesus found that Lazarus had already been in the tomb for four days. [18] Now Bethany was less than two miles from Jerusalem, [19] and many Jews had come to Martha and Mary to comfort them in the loss of their brother. [20] When Martha heard that Jesus was coming, she went out to meet him, but Mary stayed at home.
>
> [21] "Lord," Martha said to Jesus, "if you had been here, my brother would not have died. [22] But I know that even now God will give you whatever you ask." (John 11:18-22)

Jesus arrives-Lazarus has been dead for four days. Now the duration of his death is important. There was a Jewish superstition within that day that a soul would linger around the dead corpse for three days in hopes that the soul would enter back into the body. The fact that Lazarus has been dead for four days is to make the point that he is undoubtedly dead. There's no more chance of him coming out of this.

Upon Jesus's arrival, Martha leaves the house of mourning and goes rushing to Jesus. This is out of character for Martha. She is not the one to neglect duties or step outside the norms of the culture, and so, for her to leave the family amid the mourning period tells you that she feels upset. Do you hear what she asked Jesus? Maybe you look at what was said and see it as a definitive statement, but I see the question: "Where were you? What could have been more important? Why weren't you here?" Martha is a wreck at this moment. Her brother just died. I could even see her pounding on Jesus's chest as she asked these questions. Look at how she follows up those questions with "BUT" She transitions and she does what a lot of people do (especially church people). She says I know that even now you could still fix the situation. This is not beyond God. And do you know what she is doing? She is sharing the Sunday School answer. It is almost as if she pauses right in the middle of her tears, wipes her face, and says no, I should not be crying right now because God is good. And God is good, and He is in control, and He can do anything. The problem is not with the words she says but out of the heart she is saying them in. And within many church circles, this is the culture that gets created, the culture that says you are not allowed to grieve, feel pain, or experience sadness because God is good. One of the things for me that allows me to see God's beauty is that He does allow us to feel those things and that we do not have to pretend. God is not looking for you to pretend to be further down the journey than you are right now. As the Psalmist David beautifully wrote:

> "My sacrifice, O God, is a broken spirit;
> a broken and contrite heart
> you, God, will not despise." (Psalm 51:17)

If all you have to offer God is brokenness, guess what? He will take it—He will not turn you away.

And so, Jesus looks at Martha, demonstrating that she knows the right answer, and this is His response:

> Jesus said to her, "I am the resurrection and the life.
> The one who believes in me will live, even though

they die; [26] and whoever lives by believing in me will never die. Do you believe this?"

[27] "Yes, Lord," she replied, "I believe that you are the Messiah, the Son of God, who is to come into the world." (John 11:25-27)

Jesus responds to her theology with theology. A little puzzling because her statement that He could do anything seemed to be spot on, and to that statement, Jesus responds with: I have power over death. It is as if Jesus heard what she said, "sure, but do you really believe in your guts, your inner self, that I can do anything? Do you believe that I have power over death?"

And she says, "yes, I do."

Jesus is trying to show her, her lack of belief. Jesus is not looking for self-righteous babble. He wants genuine belief. And ultimately, what we believe gets exposed. Because when life is good, it is easy to listen to worship music in the car, it's easier to be going through your Bible in a year plan (I did not say easy, I said easier because the book of numbers is easy for no one), to show up to Church on Sunday and have the belief that "God is good all the time, and all the time God is good," but how about when everything is not great? Do we truly believe that all the time God is good? Because the valleys will expose our deepest beliefs.

Jesus goes to the tomb of Lazarus with Martha, and He tells her to roll away the stone from the tomb and this is what she says:

"But, Lord," said Martha, the sister of the dead man, "by this time there is a bad odor, for he has been there four days." (John 11:39)

Martha says, Lord we should not move the stone, he's dead, undoubtedly dead, and there will be an undoubtedly bad smell that comes out of this tomb. Did she not say earlier that "even now you could still do something about this" Now that push comes to shove, it appears that maybe those words were empty, and really this is what Jesus was exposing because look at what He says:

> Then Jesus said, "Did I not tell you that if you believe, you will see the glory of God?" (John 11:40)

Notice, He says "if you believe"... simply saying you do not really believe this. It is scary to think that you could have grown up in the church, done all the bible studies, and have all the right answers and not truly believe.

Ultimately Jesus does raise Lazarus from the dead. In the following chapter of the gospel of John, Lazarus accompanied Jesus on His ministry journey. It says that many Jews were coming to faith on the account that Lazarus was raised from the dead by Jesus (John 12:11). Why would Jesus wait two days before coming to heal Lazarus? Because Jesus had eternal purposes in that waiting.

Martha had all these feelings in the middle of her suffering, and Jesus came to instruct her with theology. To show her, her lack of belief.

But Martha is not the only sister in the story. We also have her sister Mary. And in some ways, she responds differently than Martha, and in other ways, similar, and Jesus responds very differently to Mary.

> When Mary reached the place where Jesus was and saw him, she fell at his feet and said, "Lord, if you had been here, my brother would not have died." (John 11:32)

What she says looks very similar, doesn't it? It is identical to what Martha said. But completely different posture. She falls down at Jesus's feet. This is a posture of humility and worship. She understands Jesus, she understands His power, and she really does believe in who He is, but she still mourns the death of her brother. That is to be expected. Right theology does not diminish the pain of loss, right theology just does not allow you to be crushed by pain. Evidenced in:

> [13] Brothers and sisters, we do not want you to be uninformed about those who sleep in death, so that you do not grieve like the rest of mankind, who have no hope. (I Thessalonians 4:13)

Paul does not say that death should eliminate our grieving, but he does say that for the believer death does not diminish our hope.

And so, if no one ever has, can I just give you permission to feel the weight of your pain? I love the phrase that Pastor Matt Chandler coined:

> "It's okay not to be okay—
> but it's not okay to stay there." (Matt Chandler; Gospel Coalition Article; I'm (NOT) Ok- You are (NOT) ok—But let's (NOT) stay that way! September 30, 2010)

Life happens, the unimaginable happens, and that is not your fault. And in the same breath, we are encouraged to not be crushed. Why? Because of Jesus.

That is where Mary is at. She is not doing good, and rightfully so. And what happens next is the reason for you memorizing your first verse of scripture:

> "Jesus wept" (John 11:35)

Jesus does not feel the need to give her an intro to the Christian faith. He does not provide her with Wayne Grudem's book on Systematic Theology. He does not point her to Bible study. Does

Jesus think those are bad things? Obviously not, with Martha, He did give her theology 101, but not here with Mary. Why? Because her belief was not the problem. The problem was simply experiencing pain over the loss of her brother.

If you have grown up in similar church circles as me, the way Jesus responds to Martha is it! That is how we do it. We need to teach people deeper depths of scripture and point them to a small group, which is the answer to the problem. But if that's all our game plan is, I believe we are short-sighted and missing the full way of Jesus. At this moment, Jesus just grieves, mourns, and weeps with Mary. Sometimes that is all someone needs because they have the belief in Jesus, and that belief is not even wavering, but they are simply mourning the loss or pain of something or someone.

And so, we feel the way we do during suffering because we are human. And the world is a broken place, and it is not wrong to feel the emotions that we do. But when these feelings rise to the place of doubting God, we have to submit our feelings and inform our feelings of truth:

> [3] For though we live in the world, we do not wage war as the world does. [4] The weapons we fight with are not the weapons of the world. On the contrary, they have divine power to demolish strongholds. [5] We demolish arguments and every pretension that sets itself up against the knowledge of God, and we take captive every thought to make it obedient to Christ. (II Corinthians 10:3-5)

Paul essentially says, "Feelings don't get to have a driver's license," not that they are not there or that they do not have a spot in the vehicle, but the moment the feelings and thoughts get behind the steering wheel and step on the gas, you have to pump the brakes and take all of them captive. And not even just take the thoughts captive—but make them obedient to Christ. How do we do this?

Well, what is interesting is that when Paul wrote those verses in II Corinthians, he was not making the instruction for our personal thoughts, but that if people were making accusations against God, putting these thoughts out in the public square that God wasn't good, or that He could not be trusted, or wasn't real...then we have to demolish those thoughts. And so, when the feelings of fear and anxiousness arise to a place that is not healthy, and we make accusations on God's power or His goodness, we have to come back and remind ourselves of the ways Jesus responded to Mary and Martha...That God is bigger than whatever I am facing in my life and that God deeply cares. Feelings are great until they are liars. We must always filter our feelings through the lenses of God's Word.

CHAPTER 4

WHEN WILL LIFE GET EASIER?

"One does not surrender a life in an instant. That which is lifelong can only be surrendered in a lifetime." Elisabeth Elliott

I am sure that growing up, you had a hero in your mind or someone you wanted to be like. In my childhood, I wanted to be like my dad. My dad was a very accomplished weightlifter, who had competed in bodybuilding shows, and I was the kid on the playground running around telling other kids about how my dad was able to beat up their dad. Most days after my dad would get home from work (delivering furniture), he would spend about an hour or two in our basement pumping iron to a shrine of Arnold Schwarzenegger and would be working out to music blaring (if you are ever in need of good workout music, I promise you that the Bee Gees will not disappoint). And occasionally, my dad would invite my brother or I downstairs to the basement to work out with him. And I remember watching him do amazing things, like filling up the bar with 45lbs. plates and doing deadlifts, and the bar would be bending (because if the bar aint bending, you are just pretending), and when he would drop the weights on the ground, the house would shake. And I remember thinking, I cannot wait till I become that big and can do those things. Well, now that I am pushing thirty, the jury is not out, but I would have to really turn gears from where I am to arrive at some of those goals. It is not hard for us to picture some level of a utopia, that once I arrive there, then life will be good and easy. Do you know the interesting thing? As large as my dad was, he never thought he was big enough, and I have met many other weightlifters who have those same thoughts. And so, the question is, do we ever arrive? Well, I guess the answer would be contingent on what we mean by the word "arrive." And if we did arrive, what do we plan on receiving upon arrival?

You see, now that I am older—I have seen certain aspirations change, as I am sure is true for you as well. And sure, do I personally think the ability to lift such heavy weights that a house would shake when they drop would be cool? Yeah, that would be cool. But it is not the promised land that I am chasing.

I was recently at a Pastor's Soul care group that I attend. Now, I'm one of the younger pastors in the group, and we were doing a practice called Lectico Divina (which is simply meditating on scripture and treating scripture like it is a living word, where God is trying to communicate to you) and the phrase that I kept meditating on was "how long Lord?" And as I really sat and thought about that question, I realized there are some areas in my own life where I can feel a tad bit restless: my marriage being one of them. Being so new to marriage, my wife Karen and I sometimes find ourselves bickering about stuff that does not matter, or we get defensive about our positions and go in circles. And so, for both of us, the thought is, when does it get easier? So much of the wisdom we have been given is "the first year's the hardest," and I am sure there is truth to that. But while I was meditating on "how long, Lord?" for me, it was—when do I arrive at being the husband that never causes my wife any grief? When is our marriage going to be void of all conflicts and disagreements? At this point, I had begun to verbalize those exact thoughts, and it seemed as though the older pastors were not sympathizing with my angst, but rather must have thought that I was performing some level of stand-up comedy because I had them rolling in laughter, however, I was not trying to be funny. I love being married, I love my wife, and yet I still want to believe that there is this eutopia in which, once we arrive, it will mean that we do not experience conflicts. If you have been married for any extended length of time, I am sure you would be able to share in the laughter. And this was just one area of my life, I would also love to arrive as a pastor, where I do not need to call mentors and ask questions about what to do and how to do it.

I think if you and I could be honest with each other, we probably have this idea in our mind that there is a way to become Superman or Wonderwoman within this life where bullets would just bounce off of us. That at some point, we will reach a level of maturity where nothing can phase us, and our life is one where struggling is absent. Whether we would say that out loud or not, that thought probably exists somewhere in the recesses of your mind. And then when struggle arrives again, or pain shows up, and you find yourself still frustrated, and the pain still hurts, what do we do?

I am reminded of what the Apostle Paul said in Romans 7

> [18] For I know that good itself does not dwell in me, that is, in my sinful nature. For I have the desire to do what is good, but I cannot carry it out. [19] For I do not do the good I want to do, but the evil I do not want to do—this I keep on doing. (Romans 7:18-19)

Paul is speaking to this war that wages between flesh and spirit. And here we have this guy, who is older now, and he had a lot of life experiences. He saw God's favor on his life. He planted churches, preached sermons, and became a father in the faith (so to speak; for Timothy) and you know what he concludes—the struggle is real, and it does not vanish this side of eternity. And within this context, Paul wants to know why he has not yet experienced power over sin in his flesh.

But for some of us, we want to know why we have not seen the power over sin when:

- When we snap at our spouse
- When we cannot stop looking at pornography
- When we cannot stop abusing substances

And the list could continue, but we want to see the struggle stop because of the pain or frustration that comes from the struggle. And it is easy to think that life is not supposed to be this way. When you get married and you make your vows, you say those things not thinking about the difficulties that are ahead of you: for better or for worse, well certainly worse is not in our future, we do not like to imagine the worst of the two, but what if you do end up sick? And what if you do end up poor? I have met with handfuls of couples who struggle to get pregnant or find out that they cannot get pregnant, which is a heavyweight, and I have met with couples who financially struggle and wonder when the finances will be all taken care of.

We are constantly looking for arrival, believing that then everything will be all right when we arrive. Pastoral ministry was not always the plan for me. Upon exiting high school, I had high hopes of going into the United States Navy, and that was the plan for me. I knew that I was going to need a medical waiver to enlist because of the Crohn's Disease diagnosis, but there was nothing I wanted to do more than to serve my country, and to be like a modern-day Rambo (every movie at that time was Hollywoodizing the military). And before graduation, I was hit with the news that I would not be able to receive a medical waiver because my condition was worse off now than it was when I was originally diagnosed. I could not believe this—I was not even feeling any symptoms. I received the news from waking up from a cat scan, and I honestly thought I was still dreaming, and I could not wait to wake up from this nightmare. To no avail, this was my reality. Leaving high school, I was confused as to what was next because I was not a serious student. In my mind, college was not on the table, so I filled out an interest card with the Detroit Police Department. Lo and behold, they called me in for an interview and gave me the rundown of all that I would need to do to become a Detroit Police Officer. And so I went and completed some tests, both written and physical, called MCOLES, and then I did a ride-along in the city of Detroit, it was non-stop action the entire night, and it was everything I wanted as a nineteen-year-old guy. Fast forward a couple of weeks, and I was in the heart of the city. I was at this office building to receive all this paperwork that needed to be filled out for a background check. Once this was completed, we would be moving on to the interview stage, which for me, got me excited because, at this point in my life, I didn't really have a background to get checked. I mean, I did a few immature things but nothing to get on my record. I figured I was in, and I could practically see the end in sight. I was finally going to arrive at an aspiration (or so I thought). At this time, I was still being treated for Crohn's Disease and receiving treatments. However, one Saturday morning, I went into anaphylactic shock. One second I was breathing, and the next, I was not. My chest started to puff up, and my throat started to enclose, and I began to black in and out. The nurses on-site at this medical clinic began pumping me full of steroids and oxygen and got me breathing again (this will probably be the last story that I share about almost dying). From there is where I ended up at the hospital and was told that I was going to need to go in for emergency surgery that night. That night I had a 7-hour bowel resection that I was not ready for and that surgery caused me to spend nearly two months in the hospital. And it was during that time that God really solidified a calling in my life for pastoral ministry. Now remember, I was right in the middle of pursuing law enforcement with the Detroit police department, but God had other plans for me, and grew in me a desire to be a preacher of His good news to the point where my desire was greater for pastoral ministry than it was for law enforcement. That was not an easy decision to make. I can still remember the day when I officially said yes. I could not have told you the last time I had cried previously to this moment, and I began to sob uncontrollably. It felt like I was letting go of everything I had ever wanted to obey this God-given desire.

I did not have the first clue as to what I was supposed to be doing to become a pastor. So, I called the pastor that my family and I had for the first 16 years of my life. He and I had begun to meet and read books together, and he would offer me counsel. We did this for a couple of years when one day, he came and told me that he would be cutting me loose and setting me up with an internship with a church plant in our area. I had wondered if this internship meant that I was finally going to arrive at this calling to be a pastor. Again, this idea of arrival was ever before me, and I thought I was so close. The internship did not turn out at all as I anticipated. I think I had unrealistic expectations of what that internship would be, and the experiences that I would get. I was young and naïve and thought I would be getting up on the microphone and telling people all about what Jesus had done for me. That did not happen, I was given a key to the building so that I could show up once a week to clean (and there is nothing wrong with that), but being 19 years old and full of youthful optimism, I was hoping for additional responsibilities, and I can remember one night really having it out with God, I will never forget it. It was a Friday night. I needed to get the church cleaned before the weekend began. And I was in the men's restroom cleaning, and I just stopped, and I looked around and said, "God, I gave up everything I wanted to do for this??? To clean bathrooms??? I thought you wanted me to share my testimony??? And preaching and doing all the fun things??? These few small responsibilities seemed to not be what I was saying yes to. I learned very quickly the truth of this quote:

> "Whoever can be trusted with very little can also be trusted with much, and whoever is dishonest with very little will also be dishonest with much." Jesus (Luke 16:10)

That church plant never got off the ground, and so I was on to the next step in this journey toward becoming a pastor. I was looking to get educated, and so I went to Wisconsin to do a campus visit at Bible College out there, and while I was on the campus tour, I absolutely loved it. I thought there was a lot to do on campus, the academics seemed to be good, and the dorm I stayed in, I really hit it off with the guys. Upon returning home, every day, I would go check the mailbox for my acceptance letter, and one day, I came home to a piece of mail from the school. As I opened it up, I quickly realized that it was a letter declining my admittance to the school. I was crushed. And so I went back to working at an automotive manufacturing shop, thinking that God was not opening doors for ministry for me.

Then one night, while I was working, a friend reached out to me and told me that I should come work at this Christian outdoor camp in Georgia. It did not seem ideal at the time. I was still recovering from all the roadblocks that I experienced in ministry up until this point. It was only a job for the summer, and it only paid one hundred dollars a week. I was working a job that paid substantially more than that. I was told that they would not "hold" my job but that if something was available after the summer, I would be free to apply again. There was no telling whether or not I was going to even get offered a job at this camp because hundreds of people applied for just a handful of positions. Well, I eventually got offered a position, and despite wise counsel around me, several people between family and friends told me that this camp was not going to be a good idea for me. I went. I absolutely loved my experience at that camp. It was honestly hard for me to leave. I think I might have even shed a few tears on the way home.

What that camp experience did for me was it reignited my knowledge that God wanted me to be in pastoral ministry, and so upon coming home, I knew that I just needed to plug into a church, a church that was going to let me serve and gain valuable ministry experience. God opened that door too, a very large church in my area back at home was doing internships and they were really built out, and so I had begun to serve within a very large college/young adult ministry as an intern, and I was being poured into by the leadership. I was doing usual internship stuff (running to the store to pick up things like coffee and balloons), and eventually, I got opportunities to preach and those preaching opportunities led to being able to go on trips to India to teach. God had really begun to open door after door where I once thought the road was closed.

At the beginning of the pandemic, March of 2020, I received a call from the pastor who I had all throughout my childhood and teen years and was the one who originally met with me after I had felt called into the ministry. And on this call, he shared with me that there was a church that was in decline and wanted to know if I wanted to plant a church out of the building with the existing church members. I went through praying, discerning, and seeking Godly, wise counsel before saying yes, but that is ultimately what happened. Three years later, I am still pastoring the church, and I can remember once I said yes to coming and being the lead pastor, and the church voted me in. It was like I had finally arrived. And if, upon arrival, I was supposed to receive a life free of struggles, that would be laughable. I was talking with a pastor friend the other day. I shared how this has been the hardest thing I have ever done. I have faced challenges that I never thought would come about. Despite the difficulties I have faced in "arriving," there have been some amazing experiences since becoming a pastor.

It is as if Solomon was right when he wrote:

> There is a time for everything,
> and a season for every activity under the heavens:
> ² a time to be born and a time to die,
> a time to plant and a time to uproot,
> ³ a time to kill and a time to heal,
> a time to tear down and a time to build,
> ⁴ a time to weep and a time to laugh,

a time to mourn and a time to dance,
[5] a time to scatter stones and a time to gather them,
a time to embrace and a time to refrain from embracing,
[6] a time to search and a time to give up,
a time to keep and a time to throw away,
[7] a time to tear and a time to mend,
a time to be silent and a time to speak,
[8] a time to love and a time to hate,
a time for war and a time for peace. (Ecclesiastes 3:1-8)

I love the book of Ecclesiastes because it is just so real. You have Solomon, arguably one of the wealthiest individuals to ever walk the face of the planet, and he conducts this grand case study where he wants to know how much he can acquire until he eventually "arrives" at the place where suffering isn't present. And he said this pursuit was meaningless. What is so amazing about that conclusion was that this was not a guy who just got fired from his job, divorced from his spouse, or had to declare bankruptcy. He is a guy who was experiencing more wealth than you will ever have, getting more action in the bedroom than you'll get in your lifetime, he had bigger parties than you've been to, and he never arrived at a life free of difficulty, and his wealth never made him immune to hard things. Under the sun, we experience all kinds of seasons that fill us with joy and seasons that are really hard and difficult that we would have never wished for, and there is not a class that you can take. There is not a status that you can get to that would make you immune to hardships.

However, there is really good news, good news for today and good news for tomorrow. I remember when I was in the hospital, a verse that provided me much comfort was found in the book of Philippians:

Rejoice in the Lord always. I will say it again: Rejoice! (Philippians 4:4)

I thought that rejoicing was something you did when something good was happening to you. But that was not the case for Paul in the midst of his command to rejoice. At this time, Paul was in prison, he was never one to deny the reality he was in, and yet he says to "rejoice." If I was on the other end of that command (oh wait, I am), but if I was Paul's original audience, I would be scratching my head at a command like this. Because my mind would immediately run to circumstances and think you do not get to control those. Therefore, you do not get to control your ability to rejoice. Later on in Philippians 4, Paul is going to show us that rejoicing is not predicated on circumstances and that he is not even asking you to rejoice in your circumstances. He says to rejoice in the Lord. Because whether your life is on the mountain top right now or in the valley, rejoicing is difficult. When life is hard, it is pretty self-explanatory why it is difficult to rejoice. But it is also hard to rejoice in the Lord when you have a lot because initially, your rejoicing wants to be in your circumstances/or objects, and once you realize that stuff and people make crummy gods, you will find it hard to rejoice in the Lord. I mean, when you look through the whole Old Testament in the Bible, God's chosen people NEVER do well with prosperity. It never turns them into deeper worshippers of God. And even in our modern context, is not Hollywood the prime example? Look at some of these quotes. I am sure you will recognize some of the names:

> "I think everybody should get rich and famous and do everything they ever dreamed of so they can see that it's not the answer." Jim Carrey

> "I've been hanging around a lot of people that are wealthy, that is rich, that is famous. One thing I learned is that no matter how much money you have, no matter how big you are, how famous you are, they will still end up stealing your charger and your lighter." Cardi B

I don't care too much for money. Money can't buy
me love– The Beatles

No matter what we are experiencing, rejoicing in the Lord can feel laborious. Paul lets us in on something, though, on how we might be able to experience the ability to rejoice.

Specifically, Paul is talking about finances, but this principle carries itself outside of finances:

> [11] I am not saying this because I am in need, for I have
> learned to be content whatever the circumstances. [12]
> I know what it is to be in need, and I know what it
> is to have plenty. I have learned the secret of being
> content in any and every situation, whether well-
> fed or hungry, whether living in plenty or in want.
> (Philippians 4:11-12)

Paul makes a comment in v.11 about contentment, and that he has arrived at that place, that he can face any situation and know that he is content. And he says he knows that through experience, he says that there have been times in his life that were really good. I would imagine that when he got invited to stay in Lydia's household in Acts 16, that he was experiencing what it was like to be upper class, but he can also think about times (like the one he is in while writing this letter to the church at Philippi, where he is in prison) and anything can come at him because he is content.

And maybe that is what your hope is with, wondering when life is going to get easier. Because I am sure you are a rationale human and know that between now and eternity, you will experience difficulties (I mean, even Jesus promised us hard times. "In this world, you WILL HAVE tribulations….but take heart I have overcome the world" John 16:33) but you just want to be able to know that you have a head above water amidst the storm.

Well, in verse 12, Paul says, "I know the secret"…I always hate when someone mentions that they know a secret because what is the point of telling us that you have a secret if you are not going to share? Tell us the secret, Paul!! Thankfully, he does. Thankfully, he shares the secret of knowing how to endure any and all seasons:

> I can do all this through Him who gives me strength (Philippians 4:13)

Paul says you want to know my secret of why I have not lost my mind while I am down here in the dungeon? It is Christ- it is a joy that is found in Him, and it is a joy that has stood the test of time, and this was not some pie-in-the-sky answer that Paul is giving to the church at Philippi or us today. Paul found the joy of following Jesus, so much so that he says this in Chapter 1:

> "For to me to live is Christ and to die is gain. (Philippians 1:21)

Paul believed and knew that because of the life that he found in Jesus—that the worst thing someone could do to him (kill him) was actually a gain. Which made Paul the impossible man to deal with—Rome had their hands full with a guy who thought death was victory. Because Paul knew that whenever God determined to bring him to Heaven, that then, and only then, his soul would truly "arrive." Because look at this descriptor of Heaven:

> "Then I saw "a new heaven and a new earth," for the first heaven and the first earth had passed away, and there was no longer any sea. I saw the Holy City, the new Jerusalem, coming down out of heaven from God, prepared as a bride beautifully dressed for her husband. And I heard a loud voice from the throne saying, "Look! God's dwelling place I snow among the people, and he will dwell with them.

They will be his people, and God himself will be with them and be their God. 'He will wipe every tear from their eyes. There will be no more death' or mourning or crying or pain, for the older order of things has passed away." (Revelation 21:1-4)

That sounds amazing, doesn't it? Eternity in the presence of God and the absence of what? Struggle, pain, hardships and suffering. And so, the beauty of Jesus is that He is good news for today and tomorrow. Jesus offers contentment today, the ability to keep your head above water and to endure the storm.

"I have learned to kiss the wave that throws me up against the rock of ages," Charles Spurgeon.

Jesus affords us that the strength to know that nothing we are enduring now, whether difficult or easy, will be wasted. And not only does Jesus afford us contentment for the now, but he affords us the fullness of eternal life in Heaven with God forever. Jesus is the way, the truth, and the life—and so, arrival happens upon knowing, loving, and worshipping Jesus despite what you may be facing.

CHAPTER 5

GOD, DON'T YOU CARE?

The matters we or the world might consider trivial, He cares about and wants to remedy. He longs to relieve our worries and has promised to supply our most fundamental needs. - Author: Charles R. Swindoll

A good friend of mine named Justin is an incredible fine artist, and it always amazes me when I see the paintings that he does. When Justin first began at art school, I was just returning home from the camp I worked at in Georgia. I had some photos from the summer that I thought had amazing views. So he offered to do a painting for me, and all I had to do was pay for the canvas and supplies (I don't think I would get that deal anymore). So, of course, I went ahead with that deal and I remember giving him the photo I wanted painted. Now quick disclaimer, I am not a fine artist. I am convinced I would mess up numbered water color paintings, and so that should tell you how little I know about the process. With my limited knowledge, I believed that this painting was taking a long time to get done (artists always have multiple projects going on), and I would stop by to see the progress every couple of days, and then I remember seeing big blobs of paint that did not make sense to my untrained eye. After one visit, I was driving home thinking, does Justin even care about this painting? It is taking him forever, and it does not appear that he is doing a good job. I wondered why? Was it just that all the other paintings were just more important? Ultimately, the painting came out to be a masterpiece. In my not knowing, I had made conclusions about whether or not my friend cared.

It can be easy to adopt this way of thinking when we think about God. After all, God has so many things to take care of and be mindful of. My circumstances can feel so small and insignificant with everything going on in the world.

Do you realize how big the universe is?

If you were to travel around the "observable" universe (because the universe transcends even what we are capable of observing) at the speed of light, it would take you 93 billion years to make the trip around. My head hurts even thinking about that distance. And Jesus is King over all of the universe. This is a quote from Abraham Kuyper:

> "There is not a square inch in the whole domain of our human existence over which Christ, who is Sovereign over all, does not cry, Mine!" (*Abraham Kuyper: A Centennial Reader*, ed. James D. Bratt (Eerdmans, 1998), 488).

The world is so big, and its problems are so vast, and that reality-it can lead us to question, how could God ever care for me? Surely He is more busy solving world hunger or human sex trafficking, and surely He cares or is more involved in the lives of world leaders, and what we can do is minimize our hurts and pains.

> [3] When I consider your heavens,
> the work of your fingers,
> the moon and the stars,
> which you have set in place,
> [4] what is mankind that you are mindful of them,
> human beings that you care for them? (Psalm 8:3-4)

David looks up at the milky way and he is blown away by God. Do we marvel at God's creation in this way? Do we see it as magnificent as it really is? Louie Giglio shares this thought:

> "As Paul Hawken keenly observed, Ralph Waldo Emerson once asked what we would do if the stars only came out once every thousand years. No one would sleep that night, of course.... We would be ecstatic, delirious, made rapturous by the glory of God. Instead, the stars come out every night and we watch television." (Louie Giglio, <u>Indescribable: Encountering the Glory of God in the Beauty of the Universe</u>)

David believed that God, who transcends the heavens of heavens, was deeply aware of humanity, particularly his own life. What would it look like for you to really believe that? For David, as he went on in Psalm chapter 8—he makes the point of the value of humanity, and the intentional design that God did within mankind, and the high position that God gave to humans:

> You have made them a little lower than the angels
> and crowned them with glory and honor.
> ⁶ You made them rulers over the works of your hands;
> you put everything under their feet:
> ⁷ all flocks and herds,
> and the animals of the wild,
> ⁸ the birds in the sky,
> and the fish in the sea,
> all that swim the paths of the seas.

I think modern evangelical circles (specifically fundamentalists) have done a good job of reminding people that they are broken, but have we missed the beauty of humanity? I love how Pastor Timothy Keller speaks to this:

> "The gospel is this: We are more sinful and flawed in ourselves than we ever dared believe, yet at the very same time, we are more loved and accepted in Jesus Christ than we ever dared hope." (Timothy Keller, <u>The Meaning of Marriage: Facing the Complexities of Commitment with the Wisdom of God</u>)

And for the most part, many Christian circles have nailed the first part of that quote, but if all people ever hear is that they are deeply broken, but they are not also taught that they are deeply loved, then church buildings will look like a prison camp to avoid, rather than a hospital to rush to. I am sure that fundamentalist circles have attempted to overcorrect circles that over-emphasize "self" as in preaching in a way that would be considered "narcigesis" and that simply is infusing self into the stories as if self is the hero, when clearly Jesus is. But often, in an effort to correct, people will overcorrect and swing the pendulum far too much in the other direction. And maybe you are reading what I just wrote and wondering, does he think that humanity is not sinners, fallen, broken--I believe all of that to be true. I believe that we are born with a sinful nature (Psalm 51:5; Romans 5:12), and yet, I believe we have value and beauty. Think of it like this, if I had a crisp, fresh off-the-press one-hundred-dollar bill and asked you if you wanted that, your answer would be "absolutely." Now answer me this, if I took the one-hundred-dollar bill and crinkled it all up, spat on in, stomped on in, ran it through some dirt, and then followed up with on whether or not you still wanted the money, I am just going to guess that you would still want that hundred dollars. I will take it a step further. Even if I ripped the bill in half, my guess would be that you would see that and still want the now-torn bill. We need to be careful not to devalue anything (especially humans) which God has created.

Depending on how you were raised, and if you were raised that God was this Santa Claus-esk figure who was just watching your every move, and he was making a list and checking it twice, ready to punish you for being naughty, or a Zeus like figure who was going to hit you with a lightning bolt for sinning, then you do not have difficulty believing that God is mindful or cares about your behavior. Then when we talk about whether God cares, it does not take much convincing to think that God does care about morality and sin. My point is not that God does not care about those things. I believe He does care about sin. I believe He does care about morality that flows from the heart. But I also have the understanding that God is slow to anger and abounding in steadfast love. I love how Eugene Peterson has paraphrased the Bible, called the message. He paraphrases Psalm 103:6-18

> God makes everything come out right;
> he puts victims back on their feet.
> He showed Moses how he went about his work,
> opened up his plans to all Israel.
> God is sheer mercy and grace;
> not easily angered, he's rich in love.
> He doesn't endlessly nag and scold,
> nor hold grudges forever.
> He doesn't treat us as our sins deserve,
> nor pay us back in full for our wrongs.
> As high as heaven is over the earth,
> so strong is his love to those who fear him.
> And as far as sunrise is from sunset,
> he has separated us from our sins.
> As parents feel for their children,
> God feels for those who fear him.
> He knows us inside and out,
> keeps in mind that we're made of mud.
> Men and women don't live very long;

like wildflowers they spring up and blossom,
But a storm snuffs them out just as quickly,
leaving nothing to show they were here.
God's love, though, is ever and always,
eternally present to all who fear him,
Making everything right for them and their children
as they follow his Covenant ways
and remember to do whatever he said.

A revelation of God's character that looks much different than a graceless, no-mercy god who is Zeus like. Even a God of grace shows us a level of which God is involved, that He knows what He is forgiving us from.

And this mindset (that God is angry and ready to punish) often leads people to run from Him. Think about the Garden of Eden and Adam and Eve when sin first shows up in the story. God had created this world in perfect harmony, and then Adam and Eve sinned, they took the forbidden fruit and then this happens:

Then the man and his wife heard the sound of the Lord God as he was walking in the garden in the cool of the day, and they hid from the Lord God among the trees of the garden. [9] But the Lord God called to the man, "Where are you?"

> [10] He answered, "I heard you in the garden, and I
> was afraid because I was naked; so I hid." (Genesis
> 3:8-10)

Once they sinned and realized that God was coming near them, it says that they hid, and when God asks Adam, why are you hiding? Adam's response was, "I was afraid." They felt ashamed for sinning, and so sin led to shame, fear, and hiding. And that same cycle has followed mankind ever since. There is this story in the New Testament that John records about this woman from Samaria. The full story can be read in John chapter 4. But as Jesus was going about

His ministry, there was this instance where Jesus intentionally went to cross paths with this woman of Samaria, and so they met at this well (undenounced to the woman), but Jesus showed up to the well when it was not busy, and there was this woman there, and she was there because she did not want to be around people in that town because of the reputation that she had (essentially she was looking to avoid the looks and snickers) and Jesus begins having this dialogue with her, and what Jesus is trying to do is show her that God's love is greater and can offer true satisfaction to the soul, that nothing else in the world can, and He point blank asked her, do you want this? Do you want to truly experience God's love? This was the point in the message where there is an alter call. If you grew up in the church, this is when the preacher says, "Every head bowed, and every eye closed," and do you know what she does? She raises her hand. She is ready to sign the card, and join a small group, the whole nine. Look at the response Jesus has for her:

> He told her, "Go, call your husband and come back." (John 4:16)

By almost all accounts, people would look at what Jesus just did and say that he messed it up. Here was this woman who was ready to pray the sinner's prayer, and instead of Jesus showing her or telling her what to pray—he says for her to "Go get your husband." This does not make a whole lot of sense. And yet, Jesus is doing something profound here. Because look at this quick dialogue:

"I have no husband," she replied.

> Jesus said to her, "You are right when you say you have no husband. [18] The fact is, you have had five husbands, and the man you now have is not your husband. What you have just said is quite true." (John 4:17-18)

The woman, in an attempt to self-protect and to not add shame, she determines it would be better to hide this area of her life. Maybe you would read this story and think Jesus needs to mind his business. If she does not want to talk about it, then Jesus should respect that. Now in many cases, I agree with that thought, but in this very moment, Jesus is trying to show her that he knows why she is hiding. He knows why she is showing up to the public well at midday as opposed to the morning with everyone else. She felt shame about her past and present relationships with men, and she believed that it was these things that made her unlovable or unworthy.

We can do this too; it is called a false self. A false self is a façade we put on in order to belong, but it is not who we really are. And so, she is doing all the things to belong- she is trying to say the right answers, and she is trying to hide anything that she believes would hinder God's love for her. Because we put the false self on, because we believe that is what is necessary to be worthy of love. It is not hard for us to believe that God loves and cares about us when life is going great, and we have an amazing quiet time with God, and in our Bible in a year plan, and only listening to Christian music, and not saying four-letter words that we ought not to say. It is not hard to believe that God can love me, but to believe that God loves me even in my mess, my brokenness, and my sin, that can be hard to wrap the mind around. And that is what Jesus is showing the woman at the well, that in order for her to be loved fully, she needs to know that she is fully known. Jesus says I know about the guy thing, and I love you, and if you do not know that I know about the five husbands, you will only believe that your false self is worthy of love. Jesus gives this woman His first "I am" statement (revelation of His divinity) within the gospel of John. You would think that He would have given it to the motley crew of guys that left everything to follow him or even possibly an influential religious leader like Nicodemus in John chapter 3 who comes asking Jesus questions in the middle of the night. But no, the first I am statement was given to this broken woman:

The woman said, "I know that Messiah" (called Christ) "is coming. When he comes, he will explain everything to us."

> [26] Then Jesus declared, "I, the one speaking to you—I am he." (John 4:25-26)

Jesus told her the one you are talking about, you are talking to. This story beautifully depicts how God cares about our brokenness, even the things we would rather not talk about, the things we would rather hide from God, He knows, and He cares, but not in a way that He is looking to condemn but rather looking to heal and save.

This story would let us know that God cares about our relationship with him, but it does not necessarily give us the hope that He cares about our suffering and our pain.

Have you ever just sat there and thought about what God is thinking about? What does God care about? What is He actively doing right now?

Do you know that God prays for you in the person of the Holy Spirit? Look at this:

> [26] In the same way, the Spirit helps us in our weakness. We do not know what we ought to pray for, but the Spirit himself intercedes for us through wordless groans. [27] And he who searches our hearts knows the mind of the Spirit, because the Spirit intercedes for God's people in accordance with the will of God. (Romans 8:26-27)

The Apostle Paul writes that God searches our hearts. He knows exactly what is that you are going through, he knows the feelings that you have, he knows the hurts you have gone through, and God has His spirit pray for us, and it is not just that He prays for us, but it says that He prays for us when we do not know what to say. When you have reached that point of frustration and hurt and being puzzled, and you do not even know what you should pray for, God steps in. That tells me that God understands our hearts more than we do. He sees the deepest recesses that we merely wonder at. And He has a plan.

I love this story that Luke tells us about when Jesus went over to His friend's house for a dinner party:

> [38] As Jesus and his disciples were on their way, he came to a village where a woman named Martha opened her home to him. [39] She had a sister called Mary, who sat at the Lord's feet listening to what he said. [40] But Martha was distracted by all the preparations that had to be made. She came to him and asked, "Lord, don't you care that my sister has left me to do the work by myself? Tell her to help me!" (Luke 10:38-40)

These sisters seem to pop up a lot within Jesus's ministry, but they are obviously close, and Jesus gets invited into their home. And as the night is underway, we see that the sisters take on two different postures. Mary sits at the feet of Jesus and is discipled by His teaching. While Martha is getting all the preparations made for the night, I'm sure that is getting the house in order, finishing up the dinner (and when you have Jesus in the house for dinner, you go a little beyond the jar of spaghetti sauce) and I am sure you could imagine that tension is building for Martha, as she is the one who is doing all the work, while Mary has this front row seat with Jesus. And her frustration hits a point, so she says to Jesus, "Lord, don't you care?" Do you see what she said by asking that question? She makes an accusation against Jesus because you would not ask someone "don't you care" if you thought that person cares, you only ask that question out of the assumption that they do not...I can see tears in her eyes as she asks the question... and because of how Jesus responds...my best understanding of this text as I have been studying it...is that Martha is asking this question out of a deep hurt. Because it is amid her frustration and hurt....

that she is so hurt that she does not even go up to Mary and say something…. She goes up and says to Jesus, "you tell her to help me" …it's almost as if she is feeling left out…

Like she's saying, "Lord don't you care that I'm not with you" "Don't you care that I have all these things keeping me away from you?"

And so let's think about some of the things that maybe have kept you from coming and being with Jesus… "Lord, don't you care that I'm depressed?"

"Lord, don't you care that my anxiety is through the roof?"

"Lord, don't you care that I self-harmed myself last week?"

"Lord, don't you care that I have all of these suicidal thoughts?"

"Lord, don't you care that my relationship or marriage is destroyed?"

And so, this is where Martha is at…she's trying her best to get everything done and keep a level head, and it's just hard, and then she's looking at her sister, and she has seemingly no worries and is just enjoying life. And maybe that's where you're at. You've got a million and one things you are trying to juggle, there are frustrations and hurts happening in your life, and you feel unseen and unwanted and then when you look around, you see that everyone else is living the high life and they have no problems….and you can just begin to feel forgotten. I think that is where Martha is, so I feel sorry for Martha because I can sympathize with her. There were many nights for me where I was in that hospital bed making those same accusatory statements (God, why do you not care?). In those moments of feeling not seen, these accusatory thoughts can feel all too real. I do not know about you, but I can become quite defensive if someone comes at me, making accusations about my character and care. Jesus does not do that, though. He would have been very justified to fly off the handle and say, "how dare you," but in love, this is how He responds:

> "Martha, Martha," the Lord answered, "you are
> worried and upset about many things (Luke 10:41)

Here is why I know that Martha was flustered and speaking out of a hurt because look at what Jesus says, "Martha, Martha." When you see a name repeated in the New Testament, it's almost always implying a level of compassion and sensitivity. And so, what Jesus is not doing here, is he's not flying off the handle and yelling "Martha, Martha" but instead with a voice of compassion, He sees a friend who's hurting "Martha, Martha" you are anxious and troubled about many things…look what Jesus just did…he first responds with compassion, and then he acknowledges her hurt…He says I see it…I see the things that are troubling you…and so in the midst of your hurt and distractions, Jesus is saying:

> "I see that depression."
> "I see those suicidal thoughts."
> "I see your relationship trauma."
> "I see your job situation."

Could you imagine—that as you make accusations against God for him not caring or seeing what you are going through, and His response was no, no, no. I see that. I see what you are going through and I understand that these things hurt and that you are puzzled. But you do not have to be. Jesus says:

> but few things are needed—or indeed only one.
> Mary has chosen what is better, and it will not be
> taken away from her." (Luke 10:42)

Look at what Charles Spurgeon once said in regards to Martha not sitting at the feet of Jesus:

> "Imagine not that to sit at Jesus' feet is a very small,
> unmeaning thing. It means peace, for they who
> submit to Jesus find peace through his precious
> blood. It means holiness, for those who learn of

Jesus learn no sin but are instructed in things lovely and of good repute. It means strength, for they that sit with Jesus, and feed upon him, are girded with his strength; the joy of the Lord is their strength. It means wisdom, for they that learn of the Son of God understand more than the ancients because they keep his statutes. It means zeal, for the love of Christ fires hearts that live upon it, and they that are much with Jesus become like Jesus so that the zeal of the Lord's house eats them up." (Spurgeon)

Essentially, Jesus was telling Martha that she was missing out on so much had she done what Mary did. Because Jesus is the one who came to deal with our frustrations and our hurts, He was the one who came to bridge the gap between humanity and God. It is as if while Jesus was on the way to the cross, he was saying to the lost and broken world, the people who thought that God did not care about them, "I see you. I am coming for you. I will give up my life to prove that to you."

fixing our eyes on Jesus, the pioneer and perfecter of faith. For the joy set before him he endured the cross, scorning its shame, and sat down at the right hand of the throne of God. [3] Consider him who endured such opposition from sinners, so that you will not grow weary and lose heart. (Hebrews 12:2-3)

The author of Hebrews tells us to consider how much Jesus cares by how much Jesus suffered. If that is the scale of measuring, we do not have enough of an imagination to truly understand then just how much Jesus cares.

Again, depending on churches you have gone to or voices that have influenced your understanding of God, we often can think that God only cares about _____ (spiritual things) or (physical things) and they talk in terms of either/or instead of both and. And people's belief about what God cares about informs so much of how ministry is done. If someone only thinks that God cares about the spiritual, they will be right in the middle of downtown in a big city with a microphone and speaker and telling everyone walking by about how they are going to Hell, even while someone who is homeless may be walking by them desiring a meal. On the reverse end, if someone only believes that God cares about the physical may get really involved with humanitarian efforts and send foreign aid for things like food, water, clothing but fail to ever tell people about the love of God that is found in Jesus. If you can tend to find yourself falling into either of one of those camps, consider the story of Jesus and the paralytic, found in Mark 2.

Jesus had entered Capernaum, and once word got that Jesus had arrived, the masses flooded to where he was so that they could hear his teaching. It says the place was so packed that even the standing room was gone outside the door. And the story tells us that these four friends came to the place where Jesus was at, and they brought with them a man who was paralyzed. They must have heard stories of Jesus healing people and thought if I can just get to Jesus. And it says that they could not get to Jesus because the crowd was too great. Again, I am sure many of us have felt this way about Jesus, that there is just too much other stuff that has Him preoccupied. You gotta love these friends, though. They have persistence. I mean, I would personally not take no for an answer either because who knows how long these guys had carried this paralyzed man, but even if it was a couple of blocks, for me, I am looking for Jesus to settle this. And so the friends climb up onto the roof, and they dig a hole into the ceiling so that they can lower their friend through the roof.

And as the friends lower this guy through the roof, look at what Jesus says:

> [5] When Jesus saw their faith, he said to the paralyzed man, "Son, your sins are forgiven." (Mark 2:5)

I am sure the guys that lowered this man through the roof were looking for Jesus to say something different. Like what do you mean by "your sins are forgiven"? How about doing some surgery on his legs so that he can get up and walk? Jesus needed to start here so that people would know of the power He actually possessed. By Jesus forgiving sins, it caused the religious elite there to begin muttering to themselves, "Who does this guy think he is?" "Does he think he is God?" Jesus does this cool Jedi mind trick and responds to the thoughts that those guys were having and says this:

> [8] Immediately, Jesus knew in his spirit that this was what they were thinking in their hearts, and he said to them, "Why are you thinking these things? [9] Which is easier: to say to this paralyzed man, 'Your sins are forgiven,' or to say, 'Get up, take your mat and walk'? [10] But I want you to know that the Son of Man has authority on earth to forgive sins." So he said to the man, [11] "I tell you, get up, take your mat and go home." [12] He got up, took his mat and walked out in full view of them all. This amazed everyone and they praised God, saying, "We have never seen anything like this!" (Mark 2:8-12)

Jesus essentially was saying for everyone looking on—before you can believe that I can heal this man's legs, you need to understand that I have even greater power. I have power to forgive sin. Jesus was indeed making the point that He was God. And within this story, Jesus demonstrates that God cares for both the spiritual and the physical. He says do not let this just be an opportunity to get your physical healing, you need spiritual healing, you need the forgiveness of sins, but Jesus also offers the physical healing and tells the paralyzed man to get up and walk, which would be a very cruel joke if Jesus did not have the power to heal nor care to heal this man's paralysis.

For all I know, you could be going through the wringer, and you could be praying 3 times a day, 5 times on Sundays, and you are begging to God to come through for you, and your lack of hearing has led you to believe that God does not care. Friend, I deeply encourage you to look at the cross of Jesus Christ. It was on that cross where Jesus displayed the clearest form of His care. He came to offer you life and life more abundantly (John 10:10). God knows and sees all that you are and all that you are going through or have been through and wants that intimacy with you, so much so that He sent Jesus into the world to pay for sin and reconcile you to God forever. If you want to know how much God cares, look at how much Jesus suffered so that He may know you and love you forever.

CHAPTER 6

WHERE DO I GO FROM HERE?

"If you lose faith, you lose all." - Eleanor Roosevelt

Growing up, I was not much of a runner. I enjoyed playing sports like basketball, but I was not someone who went out for a five-mile run because I would have found some joy in that activity. However, shortly after graduating from High School, I was working for an automotive manufacturing company and the company was offering a deal to the employees to sign up for a half marathon, and not only was the company going to cover the cost of registration, but they were also going to pay for you to go through a training program, but wait there is even more, the company sweetened the deal by offering you to get out of work a half hour early (paid) because you were going to be headed off to your training. The deal was too sweet to pass up, and I took it; even though I was not a runner, certainly I would figure out how to become one. Prior to the training program, I do believe there was never a time when I ran a distance further than three miles, and so every run in the training program that was longer than three miles was a new personal record. The training program lasted for four months, and at the beginning, I did not believe 13.1 miles was going to be possible, and then throughout the training, I really got to the point of believing that distance was not going to be possible. I ended up going on a group run one night and it was a long run at the point within the program and it was a seven-mile run, I can hardly remember who I was with, what was talked about on the run, but I remember one thing very vividly—pain! My bones felt like that they just got hit by a car and I was still going to have to go into work that night, and so, I talked with a family friend that managed the shop at which I worked, and so I was able to stop by his (which was close to our work) and I crashed on his basement couch for a couple of hours. And as I was laying there on the couch, I began smelling something that smelled like it was burning, and then I began to hear the loudest beep, beep, beep. Honestly, my first initial thought was that there was a fire, and I was laying there in so much pain that I literally did not feel as though I could move. Well, there was only one option—I was meant to go down with the house (kidding). But honestly, I did not know what was going to happen because I was hurting so bad, and the thought of getting up and moving seemed miserable. Then the basement door opened up, and the message that was said down the stairs was, "Tyler, do you want any brownies?" That is always a great question to be asked, but it does not get any sweeter than when you think you are going to have to run for your life, but in reality, you get to eat brownies instead. It was glorious.

But maybe for you, you are at the place of feeling like you cannot get up, and the thought of moving forward seems unimaginable, and for you, because for you, the threat is real—it is not that you are going to be met with freshly baked brownies. Pain and suffering may have rocked your world so badly that the thought of returning to work, showing up at Church, or even just being in the home around your family leaves you feeling lost, confused, and stuck. Millenia has passed since that moment in the garden with Adam and Eve, and sin entered the world. Through sin, the cosmos has experienced the curse, and yet so much confusion surrounds pain and suffering. And maybe for you, you have walked with Jesus for decades, and you know all the verses, and you could quote the 23rd Psalm and every commute you have in your car is like a worship concert, and yet, you still struggle- and in your mind, you think you should be beyond that point. I would encourage you to think about the guys who walked very closely with Jesus during His earthly ministry. When the suffering came to Jesus and Jesus predicted His death, they were confused:

> [21] From that time on Jesus began to explain to his disciples that he must go to Jerusalem and suffer many things at the hands of the elders, the chief priests and the teachers of the law, and that he must be killed and on the third day be raised to life. [22] Peter took him aside and began to rebuke him. "Never, Lord!" he said. "This shall never happen to you!" [23] Jesus turned and said to Peter, "Get behind me, Satan! You are a stumbling block to me; you do not have in mind the concerns of God, but merely human concerns." (Matthew 16:21-23)

Prior to Jesus making this prediction about His death, Him and His disciples had forgotten to bring bread on their journey, and the disciples look around and are beginning to ask the question—but how will we eat? The comment that they make is not coming from the place of "What are we going to eat?" the question came from the place of "How are we going to eat?" And Jesus looks at them and tells them, "How quickly have you forgotten? Do you not remember the 2 fish? It was only a few days ago. Jesus says, don't worry I got you. As well, Jesus had begun to ask His disciples about what people were saying about Him and whom the crowds were saying that Jesus was, and then He turned to His disciples and said, "But who do you say that I am?" and Peter responds with "You are the Christ" Bingo! Peter got it (at least for the moment) and what Jesus said next:

> [17] Jesus replied, "Blessed are you, Simon son of Jonah, for this was not revealed to you by flesh and

> blood, but by my Father in heaven. [18] And I tell you
> that you are Peter, and on this rock I will build my
> church, and the gates of Hades will not overcome
> it. (Matthew 16:17-18)

Jesus told Peter that upon this declaration of Jesus being the Christ, the Son of God, that Jesus was going to build His church, and nothing was going to stop the Church.

And I bet you can imagine, as can I, the confusion the disciples would have had. Jesus goes from saying, do not worry about bread, you saw how I provided thousands of people with free lunch with just those few loaves of bread and couple of fish, and so don't worry about where your lunch is going to come from or better yet if it is coming, I am taking care of it. Then He goes on to say I am going to build my Church and not even the gates of Hell is going to prevail against my plan. And then He says, by the way, I am on my way to Jerusalem and there I am going to suffer and die. Like hold up a moment- what about lunch?

And then when we look at another instance when Jesus foretells of His death:

> 22 As they were gathering in Galilee, Jesus said to
> them, "The Son of Man is about to be delivered into
> the hands of men, 23 and they will kill him, and
> he will be raised on the third day." And they were
> greatly distressed. (Matthew 17:22-23)

Prior to this foretelling, Jesus takes Peter, James, and John up onto a mountain and there reveals His divinity to them, Jesus allows these inner three disciples to see Him shine in His glory. And then God the Father speaks out of a cloud and says, "This is my Son, whom I love; with him I am well pleased. Listen to him!" (Matthew 17:5)

These disciples literally heard the voice of God the Father, tell them this is my Son, and then Jesus told them He was going to go die. I guess if I was His disciples I would be wondering what is it that I am supposed to believe right now?

And the third time that Jesus predicts His death to His disciples, they are literally on their way to Jerusalem. Prior to that, Jesus had done extensive teaching about His Kingdom, and I just have to imagine the listeners would have a hard time reconciling the idea of an eternal kingdom when the King then shares how He is going to die.

And imagine this. Imagine you are one of the disciples of Jesus. You are hearing him share these things about how He is going to eventually end up in Jerusalem. While He is there, He is going to die. As you are following Him along on this journey, He determines that He is going to pull off the highway onto the Jerusalem exit. I would think I would be clinching my entire body, but look at the scene of Jesus entering into the city on a donkey:

> *A very large crowd spread their cloaks on the road, while others cut branches from the trees and spread them on the road. ⁹ The crowds that went ahead of him and those that followed shouted,*
> *"Hosanna to the Son of David!"*
> *"Blessed is he who comes in the name of the Lord!"*
> *"Hosanna in the highest heaven!"*
> *¹⁰ When Jesus entered Jerusalem, the whole city was stirred and asked, "Who is this?"*
> *¹¹ The crowds answered, "This is Jesus, the prophet from Nazareth in Galilee." (Matthew 21:9-11)*

Probably not what the disciples were thinking they were walking into. And they probably felt a level of justification in their feelings thinking, "see—we knew you were not going to die! You are the King! And you are going to overthrow Rome, and we are going to be able to reign with you here and now." But as the story goes, Jesus was not wrong in His foretelling's of His death, and the same crowd that was praising Him just a few days later were shouting "crucify Him."

Jesus was arrested, tried, and crucified.

Now look what it says about the disciples during those three days:

> [19] On the evening of that first day of the week, when the disciples were together, with the doors locked for fear of the Jewish leaders, Jesus came and stood among them and said, "Peace be with you!" (John 20:19)

The first day of the week (Sunday) the disciples had been barricaded in a room all weekend. I am sure with many moments of tears and questions and a whole lot of confusion. Wondering did they hear something wrong, was Jesus a fake? A conman? And I am sure there was this question looming in the air "where do we go from here?" I mean, it was not like these guys were just fresh out of high school with no direction and no aspirations when they had begun to follow Jesus. No, these guys were solidified in their careers, and they left everything to come and follow Him. Jesus became true north for these guys and they were lost without Him, nor did they desire to go anywhere else.

There was an instance within the ministry of Jesus where he had begun preaching to great crowds and multitudes, and word was spreading. I mean, if you wanted free lunch and health care, well, you better be around when this guy Jesus shows up to your town. And in John 6, Jesus had fed this crowd of nearly 20,000 individuals, and when it all wrapped up, He was on His way to Capernaum, but the cool thing about how Jesus gets there, is He walks a few miles on the water to get there. And so, this massive crowd searches for Jesus in Capernaum and when they find Him look at what Jesus says:

> *Jesus answered, "Very truly I tell you, you are looking for me, not because you saw the signs I performed but because you ate the loaves and had your fill. John 6:26*

Jesus began to look around at the crowd and quickly noticed that there were people pursuing Him that were not coming for the right reasons, and so Jesus addresses them with, "you do not want me, you just want my stuff."

And Jesus went on his teaching to say some pretty challenging things to this crowd to see who was really in and if they really understood what they were doing:

> 53 *Jesus said to them, "Very truly I tell you, unless you eat the flesh of the Son of Man and drink his blood, you have no life in you.* 54 *Whoever eats my flesh and drinks my blood has eternal life, and I will raise them up at the last day.* 55 *For my flesh is real food and my blood is real drink.* 56 *Whoever eats my flesh and drinks my blood remains in me, and I in them.* 57 *Just as the living Father sent me and I live because of the Father, so the one who feeds on me will live because of me.* 58 *This is the bread that came down from heaven. Your ancestors ate manna and died, but whoever feeds on this bread will live forever."* 59 *He said this while teaching in the synagogue in Capernaum. John 6:53-59*

Can you imagine the disciples critique of this message? Like Jesus—you are gaining all this traction, people love the miracles, they love the stuff, they thought lunch was delightful and delicious, is that not enough? Why are you talking about people eating your flesh and drinking your blood?

Because Jesus wanted them to know that He was the gift, like He Himself, and if it was just him in the flesh, would that be enough? And this is a great question for all followers of Jesus. Like if you got to Heaven, and there were no streets of gold, and there were no crowns and jewels, or beautiful home(s) and it was just Jesus—would that be enough?

Jesus was telling the crowd, I want to know that you are here for me—and the scripture tells us that the crowd dissipates—they were just there for what Jesus could give them. They were not there for Jesus Himself. Then Jesus looks at His disciples and says, "Do you want to leave too?" Jesus gives them the out, hey, if you signed up for something and you were hoping for a different outcome you could go if you want. Here is what Peter says:

> *⁶⁸ Simon Peter answered him, "Lord, to whom shall we go? You have the words of eternal life. ⁶⁹ We have come to believe and to know that you are the Holy One of God." John 6:68-69*

Peter's response- where would we go? What is better than this? These guys were in, whether the going was good or the going was difficult. And this heart was seen all the way to the end, but that did not mean there was no moments of weakness along the way and that did not mean there was no confusion watching their King die on that cross.

And the resurrected King came and found these guys in that room. He came and met them in their moments of fear and confusion. And the first message that Jesus gave them was "Peace be with you." Jesus was telling them to let the peace of God infiltrate their hearts and minds. They no longer needed to be troubled or worried.

And as Jesus's 40 days were wrapping up (his time on earth post-resurrection) He had gathered the disciples at the mount of olives because He wanted to give one last final charge but look at what happens when the disciples arrive:

> *¹⁶ Then the eleven disciples went to Galilee, to the mountain where Jesus had told them to go. ¹⁷ When they saw him, they worshiped him; but some doubted. Matthew 28:16-17*

The exalted King is about to be giving His farewell speech—
and these disciples arrive and they cannot help but worship Jesus.
However, did you notice the little caveat that Matthew gives us? The
text says that "some doubted," and again, I really try to sympathize.
I can imagine the difficulty and world wind these guys have gone
through. Still, here you have the resurrected Jesus right in front
of you. If there is any doubt on whether or not it is him, Jesus has
already covered that up, he has allowed them to touch his wounds,
he invited them to come and see, and have the close-up (ultimately
so that they would go and tell). I do not know how Jesus did it—I
don't know how He did not fly off the handle. I don't know how he
did not rebuke their doubts and worries and say something to the
effect of "How much more do I have to do? When will you fully
believe it? What will it take? You all saw me get publicly murdered,
you knew that I was put inside of a tomb, and here I am, ever before
you. I mean, after all, did not the Apostle Paul make an apologetic
defense for the validity of the resurrection by pointing to the fact
that over 500 people were witnesses of His resurrection and they
believed in I Corinthians 15:3-8:

> *3 For what I received I passed on to you as of first
> importance: that Christ died for our sins according to
> the Scriptures, 4 that he was buried, that he was raised
> on the third day according to the Scriptures, 5 and that
> he appeared to Cephas, and then to the Twelve. 6 After
> that, he appeared to more than five hundred of the
> brothers and sisters at the same time, most of whom are
> still living, though some have fallen asleep. 7 Then he
> appeared to James, then to all the apostles, 8 and last of
> all he appeared to me also, as to one abnormally born.*

And so, if a great number of people saw and believed after Jesus
resurrected, what was the difficulty for those who were closest, who
saw all the miracles, and the healings and were even foretold how all

of this would happen? The answer is—they are human, and they just saw Jesus brutally die and was raised to life by His own Spirit. And that is the reality of the human experience. We will have doubts, even about things that we are so certain of. There will be times when my wife and I are driving and getting out of our subdivision when she will ask, "did we blow out the candle" and even if I know that I did, there will be doubts that cause me to turn back around.

And in Jesus fashion, He does not freak out about their confusion and doubts and instead says this:

> *18 Then Jesus came to them and said, "All authority in heaven and on earth has been given to me. 19 Therefore go and make disciples of all nations, baptizing them in the name of the Father and of the Son and of the Holy Spirit, 20 and teaching them to obey everything I have commanded you. And surely I am with you always, to the very end of the age." Matthew 28:18-20*

Instead of rebuking them, here is the message Jesus gives: Go tell all the world about the very thing you are struggling to believe in yourself right now. Struggling and difficulties and doubts do not disqualify us from radically loving and following and being obedient to Jesus.

In fact, Jesus, in one of the most prolific sermons that He ever gave, the Sermon on the Mount, He says this:

> *34 Therefore do not worry about tomorrow, for tomorrow will worry about itself. Each day has enough trouble of its own. Matthew 6:34*

Jesus says- I know you could be looking tomorrow and thinking about all that is going to go wrong with tomorrow, and Jesus says, "don't do that"…well, why does He say that? Because today has enough problems of its own. Jesus just gave his audience permission to focus on today's worries.

And so, how are we to do this? Knowing that chances are today I am going to need to take care of worries, doubts, fears and sufferings are going to be a part of our life. Yet, our call is to move forward into the world to be ambassadors for Christ. How do we marry these two ideas and have our pain become a platform to spread the good news of Jesus?

One author Vaneetha Risner put together a good acronym about what to do when it becomes difficult to move forward or wonder where to go next that I would like to share with you, and it is this: T.R.U.S.T. (Vaneetha Risner; Desiring God Article; When praying hurts)

Turn me from temptation. Revive me through your word. Use this pain for good. Show me your glory. Teach me your ways.

TURN me from temptation:

It makes sense that the enemy would tempt you in the middle of your pain because it is a moment where you are vulnerable, and Satan has one sole motivation, and it is to destroy you. Peter shares this:

> *[7] Cast all your anxiety on him because he cares for you. [8] Be alert and of sober mind. Your enemy the devil prowls around like a roaring lion looking for someone to devour. [9] Resist him, standing firm in the faith, because you know that the family of believers throughout the world is undergoing the same kind of sufferings. I Peter 5:7-9*

Peter reminds these saints who have scattered over persecution that has come to the Church, and he tells them of the necessity to cast your anxiety onto Jesus because "He cares for you." And the very next thing is the reason why, because you have a very real enemy, like once you become a follower of Jesus, it's like you put on this big bull's eye on your back. And Peter says this well before "Rex, from Rex-Kwan-Do" ever said it (Napoleon Dynamite reference, I pray you understood it), but you need someone watching your back at all times, and God promises to be the one who sticks closer than a brother (Proverbs 18:24)

Satan desires you to fixate on your circumstance, and make you believe that God is not good, that He cannot be trusted, and nor would He be worthy of your worship, and we have been called to resist these temptations, and to stand firm in our faith because we know whom we have believed in. When Jesus was teaching His disciples how to pray in Luke 11, He tells his disciples to pray for the power to resist temptation. Prayer is one of the ways we resist the enemy's lies. I remember one of the first times praying for that "God give me power to resist temptation"—it seems like it would just be a matter of discipline (and sometimes that is part of it), but Jesus connects the ability to resist the temptation to a spiritual matter. Another way that can help us resist temptation is-

REVIVE me through your Word:

So much of our worldview is shaped around what we consume. And as we navigate difficult days, where are we looking and listening to take our cues from? I have wondered if the mental health crisis that we are experiencing in the world is partly due to the fact we have the messages of culture through music and video ever with us, ever consuming them. But in any domain within our human experience, consumption matters. If you are trying to gain or lose weight, the consumption of food matters, what you consume would matter. If you are a student and you must take an exam- what you consume matters. You would not study Algebra if you were going to be taking a world history exam. If the doctor came in and told you that you had a disease but not to panic because they have a treatment plan that is tried and true, and as long as you followed the course of medications, you are going to be ok. Then your consumption would matter. When it comes to dating or marriage, your consumption of information on how to date well or how to have a good marriage matters. The Psalmist David said in Psalm 119:11

I have hidden your word in my heart
that I might not sin against you.

David acknowledges that if he has any chance of fighting sin, it will be a result of the fact that David had stored up God's Word in his heart. Now it does not say that David won't sin. It says that he might not sin. The only fighting chance David had was building up the Word of God in his heart. And the same is true for fighting temptation. In Matthew chapter 4, Satan sets out to tempt Jesus with three different temptations:

First Satan tempts Jesus with comfort, and Jesus responds:

> *⁴ Jesus answered, "It is written: 'Man shall not live on bread alone, but on every word that comes from the mouth of God.'" (Matthew 4:4)*

Jesus quoted from Deuteronomy 8:3, and met Satan's temptation with scripture.

Satan then tempts Jesus with safety, and Jesus responds:

> ⁷ Jesus answered him, "It is also written: 'Do not put the Lord your God to the test.'" (Matthew 4:7)

Jesus quoted from Deuteronomy 6:16, and met Satan's temptation with scripture.

Lastly, Satan tempts Jesus with power, and Jesus responds:

> ¹⁰ Jesus said to him, "Away from me, Satan! For it is written: 'Worship the Lord your God, and serve him only.'" (Matthew 4:10)

Jesus quoted from Deuteronomy 6:13, and met Satan's temptation with scripture.

And so, the consumption of God's Word allows us to resist temptation, and it also leads to life. The Psalmist wrote:

> Open my eyes that I may see wonderful things in your law. (Psalm 119:18)

There is beauty and life found in the Word of God—and we rob ourselves of enjoyment when we do not feast on the Word. When we do not cling to the Word for support, and we do not go to the Word to gasp for our next breath.

Use this pain for good:

There are so many stories in the Bible where we can look at key figures and think about how God took time to bring forth good from their circumstance. I think about David, right? He was this humble shepherd and was told that he was going to be profoundly used by God and that he was going to be king over Israel, but it was over a decade before that would come, and Saul would attempt to kill him and this tension existed the whole time. Or when Moses had to wander in the desert for 40 years before the Israelites got to enter the Promised Land. Why would God's people have to wait for that long? Because God was teaching them more of Himself—He was teaching them that He's got a plan, even when it differs from there's- I think about the moment when in Exodus 17 when the Israelites are completely surrounded by an enemy- and yet Moses sees the hand of God come through and God's promise to defeat this enemy. God was not unaware of the circumstances that His people were in, He had a plan, and most often, His plan does not coincide with our hopes and dreams. God also, through these forty years, was teaching them of His provision and that He was capable of meeting their needs. At one point in the desert, the Israelites had become so hungry that they were literally thinking back to the days of when they were in Egypt and came to this conclusion "at least back there we had bread" (paraphrase of Numbers 11:5) Can you imagine, how bad things were getting in the desert, if the fantasy playing out in the minds of the Israelites is "man, I sure do miss the good ole days of slavery." It can be so easy to think about what we do not have (I don't think anyone is blaming the Israelites for being hungry, but they began to complain about God as though He forgot about their needs). In the Israelites complaint against God not providing for them, God meets them, and He meets them with food, quail and manna (Exodus 16), and as Moses shares this good news with the people, He says this food will serve as a sign that God will be faithful to give us the Promised Land. In the waiting, God is teaching His provision. In the middle of our waiting, have we given thought to how the Lord is providing?

Or how about the story of Joseph? A guy who went through the wringer—his family sold him into slavery, he spends nearly a decade in prison under false accusations, but had he not been in the prison, he would not have had the opportunity to gain the position with Pharoah that he did. And when Joseph gets reacquainted with his family all these years later, they have this impression that they need to approach Joseph with some level of timidity (after all, these were the guys responsible for Joseph enduring great suffering) and the brothers conjure up this story, and they say "dad's final wishes were that you did not seek revenge on us for what we did to you." Who knows? Maybe Joseph's father really did leave these instructions for Joseph, but the text implies that these brothers were making this story up to save their own skin. Nonetheless, Joseph hears this request from his father and is shocked. You think I'm looking to retaliate against you guys—here is the reality, after I look back upon the selling me into slavery, and I look back on my time in prison, and look to where I am at today (2ⁿᵈ in command of all of Egypt, right behind Pharaoh) and so, here is what I know:

> You intended to harm me, but God intended it for good to accomplish what is now being done, the saving of many lives (Genesis 50:20).

God has the ability of working all things together for good (Romans 8:28) and if that is true, which I believe God does have the ability- then that means that God is able to use the most horrific of circumstances to accomplish His good plans and purposes. In

Romans 8:28, Paul connects the idea of God being able to work all things together for good- to purpose. Your pain is not without purpose. Whether you can see it now or not.

Show me Your glory:

I can remember back to sitting in the hospital and receiving text messages and phone calls from very well-meaning people that would share very kind sentiments "praying for you," "Gods got you," "You are going to be OK," "Trust in the Lord" and none of these sentiments are necessarily wrong, but in that very moment, those sentiments were not alleviating the pain I was experiencing, they were not squelching doubts that I was feeling, and they were not what I felt that I needed. I grew up in Sunday School, my first steps were in the church nursery, memorizing the verses, and singing the songs. Yes I know that Jesus loves me, for the Bible tells me so. It was not a matter of not knowing these sentiments, and believe me. I am not advocating that we do not pray for the sick, or attempt to encourage people going through pain with truth—my point is that for most of us, in the midst of the hurt, we do not just want to know, we want to experience. In my two-month hospital visit, I didn't want to just know that God cared. I wanted to feel that (and I am familiar with the "facts don't care about your feelings" and yet our feelings really do matter, for the fact that we have a God who has feelings *Matthew 9:36; Isaiah 53:3; Luke 10:21; John 11:36*)
This leads me to the words of the Apostle Paul in Philippians 3:10

> [10] I want to know Christ—yes, to know the power of
> his resurrection and participation in his sufferings,
> becoming like him in his death,

Philippians chapter 3, Paul is building out this argument of why there is no reason to put confidence in the flesh, and Paul goes on and shows you his resume:

> If someone else thinks they have reasons to put
> confidence in the flesh, I have more: ⁵ circumcised
> on the eighth day of the people of Israel, of the tribe
> of Benjamin, a Hebrew of Hebrews; in regard to the
> law, a Pharisee; ⁶ as for zeal, persecuting the church;
> as for righteousness based on the law, faultless.
> (Philippians 3:4-6)

Paul had every reason to put confidence in the flesh, and in the end, he says that his knowledge had a ceiling and that he needed something or someone to transcend his knowledge. And in v.10, Paul goes on to share that it was not enough to just know about Christ, but that he wanted to know him through the experience of transformation and becoming like Christ.

Jesus, through our suffering, may we become like you, and may we truly experience the joy of sanctification.

Teach me your ways:

For most of us, there is a great disconnect between our understanding and God's understanding. When God's plans come in contention with ours, our prayers should look like: God, help me understand what I don't understand- God, help me trust that your ways are better than mine. Because prayer is not intended to have God give us what we want, but rather, that we would align ourselves with His will (Matthew 6:10)

There is a beauty in understanding that we need God's direction because the beauty I see is that there is direction.

Proverbs 3:5-6

> Trust in the Lord with all your heart
> and lean not on your own understanding;
> ⁶ in all your ways submit to him,
> and he will make your paths straight.

One of the critiques of the Church community is that Christians are ignorant, non-intellectual and that our faith is blind. Scripture does not encourage people to live without wisdom or to not exercise intellect. The encouragement is to rely on wisdom and intellect that is beyond our own. Proverbs 3:6 tells us to lean on God's understanding.

God's truths can be leaned on and trusted in. It is a bridge that holds its weight:

> "Faith is a footbridge that you don't know will hold you up over the chasm until you're forced to walk out onto it." — Nicholas Wolterstorff, Lament for a Son

And so, knowing that we are going to go through the storms of life, and there will be days that we do not understand, and wish we could pray away, what are we to do? How do we move forward amidst the pain? Faith and Trust, knowing that your story is not over and that God is in the process of giving you good things:

> "Ask and it will be given to you; seek and you will find; knock and the door will be opened to you. [8] For everyone who asks receives; the one who seeks finds; and to the one who knocks, the door will be opened.

> [9] "Which of you, if your son asks for bread, will give him a stone? [10] Or if he asks for a fish, will give him a snake? [11] If you, then, though you are evil, know how to give good gifts to your children, how much more will your Father in heaven give good gifts to those who ask him! (Matthew 7:7-11)

CONCLUSION

For nearly the last decade, I have been on a journey to begin asking God why? And have examined that question from a variety of angles. And as I have done life with so many people, I have learned that few things in this life are universal, but one thing for certain is that we all experience pain at some point in our life, and it turns our world upside down and when that happens it will require us to re-examine, or refocus our view and understanding of God. Once our life is in turmoil, we oftentimes can find ourselves with more questions than answers—and my hope is that this book serves as a help to deepen your understanding of God in the midst of suffering. Because for much of my adult life, I believed that circumstances are what fueled feelings of security or fear. That if I was destroyed with anxiety and fear, then it must be because my circumstances were not pleasant, and on the contrary, if I was happy, then it must mean that life was going great. But I have come to learn from the Word of God and life experience that feelings of fear and security are not contingent on good or bad circumstances, but rather those feelings find their life in belief. Belief about God, belief about self, and belief about the circumstances.

There is this story in the scriptures that whether you grew up in a faith community, you have heard the reference of David and Goliath, and there are a lot of factors within the story that would give David every reason to not believe God to come through for him. If David looked at the people around him, he would have seen an entire nation back down from this giant Goliath. David was going to have to be willing to be an army of two (it was just going to be David and God on that battlefield facing this giant). Could you imagine that? The circumstance that David was up against was one where there was not another individual who was like, "Let me join you" in an entire nation. I read that, and I cannot help but wonder what faith that took, and I wonder, if you and I were put in those same shoes, would we have that level of faith and belief in God's goodness? I can answer for myself: probably not, I oftentimes, do not find myself best relating to the heroes of the scripture who did all these heroic feats, but rather, I oftentimes echo the disciples when they said, "Increase our faith" (Luke 17:5). And it can be easy to question peoples belief whether it be about God or circumstance, and we can question for a variety of reasons: is that belief legitimate? Are they faking it until they make it? Is that some spiritual façade?

And within the story of David and Goliath, there are a plethora of naysayers, people who were not championing David's belief, faith, and trust in God. As mentioned earlier, faith can be work, and it can be something we are ever trying to grow in, and what does not make it easier is when our faith is met with opposition from others. I am sure as we look at some of the people that question David's motive and belief, that we would have a difficult time recovering from said doubts.

And David said to the men who stood by him, "What shall be done for the man who kills this Philistine and takes away the reproach from Israel? For who is this uncircumcised Philistine, that he should defy the armies of the living God?"

So, first, David says to the guys next to him, hey, what's the deal that's being made? David wants in on this action! Can you believe it? David, this wee little shepherd boy is going to take on the monster Goliath???

Look what he says about Goliath- who is this uncircumcised Philistine? In that moment, David was using slang to belittle Goliath.

I am sure I probably do not need to elaborate on how that statement could be taken as slang. But in that very moment, David shares with you exactly what he believes about Goliath...in essence, it's like David is saying, who is this clown that thinks he stands a chance against God's people? Like, aww man, I'm about to wreck a fool. What David sees about Goliath is vastly different from the rest of the nation. They see terror, David sees a speck, a nat, something David isn't afraid of...why? Because of what David believes about God. Did you see that? For David, he does not see Goliath as an imposition on just any old army. Rather, this is the army of the living God. David has a real issue understanding the people here. It is evidenced in the fact that he draws the comparison and truly wonders, do people not understand that this guy is directly in opposition to God? And if they did understand that, then why would they be shrinking back?

And as David makes this point, check this out:

> [8] Now Eliab his eldest brother, heard when he spoke to the men. And Eliab's anger was kindled against David, and he said, "Why have you come down? And with whom have you left those few sheep in the wilderness? I know your presumption and the evil of your heart, for you have come down to see the battle." I Samuel 17:28

We have Eliab over hear David's comments, and look at the response, this is how you know he did not appreciate David as Gods choice...it says that Eliab's anger was kindled against David... clearly not happy with his brother, and he says, "why have you come down here?"...David, why did you show up here? Is this some attempt to gain attention? Isn't that what Eliab says? He points right at David's heart and assigns him motivation. When he says "I know the presumption of your heart" in Eliab's mind, he believes he knows that David is not sincere. And because Eliab thinks this is some gimmick, or cry for attention, he even tries to discredit David.

Look at what he says about David's 9-5 job—"whom have you left those few sheep with" hashtag hater. But in all honesty, he really is, he is trying to show David that he thinks he's nothing.

How many of us could hear that from someone who is supposed to love you? David hears this from the lips of his brother...you are nothing.

I wonder how many of us have heard these words before? From someone we loved- they are devastating...and for a lot of people, we would think this could be an offramp for David, could it not? David could be like yeah. It was a little bit silly to think that I was going to be used by God in this way....my family is right. I'm not enough. I don't know what maybe you've walked away from because of things your family or friends thought about you, said to you... and this isn't meant to offer the level of hope that a fortune cookie does...but David's view of God liberated him from the thoughts of loved ones. And maybe you come from a good home, and you've only been championed your whole life by them, but maybe other people did not believe in you...David's family was not the only naysayers. Look at this:

> And David said to Saul, "Let no man's heart fail because of him. Your servant will go and fight with this Philistine." 33 And Saul said to David, "You are not able to go against this Philistine to fight with him, for you are but a youth, and he has been a man of war from his youth."34 But David said to Saul, "Your servant used to keep sheep for his father. And when there came a lion, or a bear, and took a lamb from the flock, 35 I went after him and struck him and delivered it out of his mouth. And if he arose against me, I caught him by his beard and struck him and killed him.36 Your servant has struck down both lions and bears, and this uncircumcised Philistine shall be like one of them, for he has defied the armies of the living God."

37 And David said, "The Lord who delivered me from the paw of the lion and from the paw of the bear will deliver me from the hand of this Philistine." And Saul said to David, "Go, and the Lord be with you!" (I Samuel 17:32-37)

David approaches Saul…and volunteers himself as tribute (hunger games anyone?)! Can you imagine the laugh that Saul had… like dude, I said you killed it on the harp, not like killed it like a soldier. I don't think this is really the arena in which we can use you. Why don't you just go back to playing the harp?

Saul says David, you are just a boy. He judges him by his appearance, and his stature and his age. And then not only does he judge him by appearance, but he also judges him by comparison…. you are nothing compared to Goliath. He eats people like you for breakfast. Saul is someone in a position of authority over David saying this.

I think most of us, at some point in our lives, have looked to those who were our elders, and desired their affirmation. I remember when I got called to come pastor the church that I know pastor, I called as many pastors with white hair or lack of hair and sought out their guidance, and I wanted to be affirmed by them. I have to imagine that if David's brothers feel this way about him, he probably doesn't have the greatest of home life (especially with how you see Eliab speak to him), and typically people will look for validation outside of the home if they aren't getting it in the home. And so, to now have a boss, if you will say this…how does David keep on? What is fueling this persistence…He tells Saul, I am not taking no for an answer, because of what I believe about God. David says, I've seen God come through for me one too many times, there was this time we had a lion get after the sheep, and I defended them and we also had a bear, and likewise I defended them…and both God times God showed up, and He saved me…and so the lion and the bear were strikes one and two, and Goliath is about to be strike three…

God is too faithful…David's belief about God led him to be able to be persistent and to fight and not fall back.

So Saul says ok, you got the job.

And as the story goes:

> Then Saul clothed David with his armor. He put a helmet of bronze on his head and clothed him with a coat of mail, [39] and David strapped his sword over his armor. And he tried in vain to go, for he had not tested them. Then David said to Saul, "I cannot go with these, for I have not tested them." So David put them off. [40] Then he took his staff in his hand and chose five smooth stones from the brook and put them in his shepherd's pouch. His sling was in his hand, and he approached the Philistine. (I Samuel 17:38-40)

Saul attempts to take the matter into his hands and says I'll prepare you, I'll make you ready, I'll give you the fighting chance, and so he puts the king's armor on David…This armor is not what was qualifying David to fight Goliath. And David says this armor isn't going to work. David takes off the armor that wasn't his. Saul had a belief about the armor, and so did David. Again, they were vastly different because what fueled David's sense of security was not in weapons or external factors (like the armor)—there was no hope in those things. Saul had put much stock in the externals, and because he had his beliefs mispriotized, fear had a stronghold. And we too, will have fear take root in us, the more we put our hope in the external or in self-reliance. What armor do we need to take off? What armor have we put on that we attempt to make us believe that we matter? Are we finding our identity and worth in our job? our education, our 401k, our appearance…our house? All our little things? Like David, we must remember, critical…our identity, our value, and our ability to fulfill God's mission in and through our lives—is going to be because of God's provision.

Goliath loses…always…if Goliath was given 1000 chances against God…Goliath loses every time.

And maybe you have come into this place this morning, and you'd say…I've given God every reason to not love, to not want me, to see me as nothing. Do you know why we are so imperfect? Do you know why we've all found ourselves in messes? Because we have an enemy…that enemy leads us toward sin and death. And it is this insurmountable enemy, we'll want you to tell about David, the greater David…His name is Jesus Christ, and he came to fight our Goliath (sin and death) … here's the cool thing…. your sin doesn't compare to the love of Jesus….Jesus wins every time.

The fact that Jesus arose from the dead and the tomb was empty, He demonstrated that He had power over sin, and if Jesus makes a provision for us in our greatest of needs i.e. sin- then why would we lack belief in the smaller things (not saying that your pain and hurt is small, it is just smaller in comparison to the greatest suffering we face which is a sin nature). An old pastor friend of mine says this "If you can trust God to save you from your sin, then you can trust Him with everything else". The empty tomb reassures me of God's plans and how they are not meant to take but to give, not meant to hurt but to heal, and not meant to condemn but to forgive. All of life's "why" questions can find their answer in the empty tomb. The empty tomb is evidence that God is making a way for us to become like Jesus. The Apostle Paul taught this in Philippians 3:10:

> I want to know Christ—yes, to know the power of
> his resurrection and participation in his sufferings,
> becoming like him in his death,

Paul saw the power of the resurrection as "becoming like him in his death." It was not just enough to know Christ, but that Paul wanted to become like him. And so God takes all the good, and all the bad, and uses those moments as part of His plan to make us more like Jesus:

> And we know that in all things God works for the good of those who love him, who[a] have been called according to his purpose. (Romans 8:28)

> God takes all things and makes them beautiful in their time (Ecclesiastes 3:11)

If it's not good, then He's not done. No, He's not done with it yet- Tauren Wells (Joy in the morning lyrics).

BIBLIOGRAPHY

Chapter 1:

Spurgeon, C. H. (n.d.). "God is too good to be unkind, too wise to be mistaken; and when you cannot trace His hand, you can trust His heart." Retrieved from [(https://quotefancy.com/quote/785423/ Charles-H-Spurgeon-God-is-too-good-to-be-unkind-too-wise-to-be-mistaken-and-when-you)]

Spurgeon, C. H. (01/14/1915). "Child of God, you cost Christ too much for him to forget you." In God's Memorial of His People (Sermon).

Challies, T. (11/2/2022). "If God is not sovereign, you are not secure." In If God is not sovereign (Article).

Chapter 2:

Chambers, O. (2015). "One of the greatest strains in life is the strain of waiting for God." In Hope: A Holy Promise (p. 62). Discovery House.

Chandler, M. (2013). "Comfort is the god of our generation, so suffering is seen as a problem to be solved, and not a providence from God." In Cross.

Tada, J. E. (2003). "Sometimes God allows what he hates to accomplish what he loves." In The God I Love.

Chapter 3:

Calvin, J. (2012). "Many falsely suppose that the feelings, which God has implanted in us as natural, proceed only from a defect. Accordingly, the perfecting of believers does not depend on their casting off all feelings, but on their yielding to them and controlling them, only for proper reason." In Commentary on Acts, Volume 2.

Chandler, M. (2010, September 30). "It's okay not to be okay—

but it's not okay to stay there." In Gospel Coalition Article: I'm (NOT) Ok- You are (NOT) ok—But let's (NOT) stay that way!

Chapter 4:

Elliott, E. (1958). "One does not surrender a life in an instant. That which is lifelong can only be surrendered in a lifetime." In Shadow of the Almighty: The Life and Testament of Jim Elliot.

Chapter 5:

Swindoll, C. R. (n.d.). "The matters we or the world might consider trivial, He cares about and wants to remedy. He longs to relieve our worries and has promised to supply our most fundamental needs."

Kuyper, A. (1998). "There is not a square inch in the whole domain of our human existence over which Christ, who is Sovereign over all, does not cry, Mine!" In J. D. Bratt (Ed.), Abraham Kuyper: A Centennial Reader (p. 488). Eerdmans.

Giglio, L. (2017). "As Paul Hawken keenly observed, Ralph Waldo Emerson once asked what we would do if the stars only came out once every thousand years. No one would sleep that night, of course.... We would be ecstatic, delirious, made rapturous by the glory of God. Instead, the stars come out every night and we watch television." In Indescribable: Encountering the Glory of God in the Beauty of the Universe.

Keller, T. (2011). "The gospel is this: We are more sinful and flawed in ourselves than we ever dared believe, yet at the very same time, we are more loved and accepted in Jesus Christ than we ever dared hope." In The Meaning of Marriage: Facing the Complexities of Commitment with the Wisdom of God.

Chapter 6:

Wolterstorff, N. (1987). "Faith is a footbridge that you don't know will hold you up over the chasm until you're forced to walk out onto it." In Lament for a Son.

Printed in the United States
by Baker & Taylor Publisher Services